Parenting in the Twenty-First Century

10 Tools for Better Parenting

By Ari Novick, Ph.D. and Martine Wehr, J.D.

Parenting in the Twenty-First Century
10 Tools for Better Parenting

Book and cover design by Contusion Design (contusion.com).

ISBN 978-1-4675-5841-9

Table of Contents

Children and Stress
Children and Trauma

114 • Tool # 9
Children and Divorce
Rules for Divorcing Parents
Guidelines for Divorced Parents to Live By

118 • Tool # 10
Co-Parenting, Step parenting and Single Parenting
Co-Parenting
- Successful Co-Parenting
- General Guidelines for Co-Parenting
- Co-Parenting Team Work/Planning
- Tips for Co-Parenting

Step Parenting and Stepfamilies
- Key tasks in becoming a Step Family
- Stepfamily Challenges
- Tips for stepfamilies

Single Parenting

133 • Appendix
I. Resources
II. References

Parenting in the Twenty-First Century

Introduction

Parenting and co-parenting well is one of the biggest challenges we face as parents today. One just has to read the newspaper daily or watch the evening news to conclude that learning to be a good parent is a major challenge for most people. Lack of good parenting skills is a major factor in domestic violence, child and spousal abuse, marital conflicts, and in family fights.

This is intended to be a self-help manual for parents who need specific tools on how to better parent their children and/or co-parent their children in a divorce or blended family situation. Every parent, even the most competent, can benefit from a bit of extra help. The skills in this manual can successfully be applied in relationships, with children, and with family members.

This parenting course is not meant to be a substitute for counseling or psychotherapy. It is intended to be educational in nature to teach concrete skills, to better parent, and to be a more effective partner in raising children of all ages.

Purpose and Benefit of Course

At the end of this course, among other topics, you will have knowledge of:

1. Parent's rights and responsibilities
2. Common parenting mistakes
3. Temperament and parenting
4. Parenting styles and loving your children
5. Parenting a child with Special Needs
6. Being a good role model
7. Assertive communication for parents
8. Stress management for parents
9. Empathy training for parents and children
10. General principles of discipline
11. Boundary and limit setting
12. Dealing with sibling rivalry
13. Basic rules for divorcing parents
14. Co-parenting teamwork/challenges
15. Step-family dynamics

About the Authors:

Ari Novick, Ph.D., *is a licensed Marriage and Family therapist, and anger management and parenting expert, who has a private practice in Laguna Beach, California. He is a clinical member of the California Association of Marriage and Family Therapists. He is also a continuing education provider for the California Board of Behavioral Sciences and an approved Parenting and Anger Management provider for the Orange County Department of Probation.*

Dr. Novick has made numerous presentations on the subjects of anger management and parenting, stress management, and empathy. He has been a consultant for the Discovery Channel, A & E, Fox Television and Ricochet T.V.

Dr. Novick is also a corporate consultant and conducts workshops and seminars for corporations in both the public and private sectors.

Dr. Novick received his bachelors' degree from the University of California at Santa Barbara, his Master's Degree from Pepperdine University and his doctorate from the California Graduate Institute.

Martine Wehr, JD *is the Director of Parenting Education and a Certified Anger Management Professional for the AJ Novick Group.*

Ms. Wehr is an associate faculty member in Saddleback College's Human Services Department, teaching courses for the Community Based Corrections and Alcohol and Drug Studies certificate programs. She serves as a board member for the Drug and Alcohol Prevention and Intervention Advisory Committee.

She is also the Founder and Director of Juvenile Counseling Services, LLC, providing juvenile diversion programs, including Youth and the Law III, an Orange County Probation approved program for first time juvenile offenders.

Ms. Wehr received her Bachelor of Arts degree in Psychology and Social Behavior, Cum Laud, with an emphasis in child development, from the University of California, Irvine and her Juris Doctor degree from Whittier Law School, as a Fellow in the Center for Children's Rights.

Welcome –You're a parent!

You are a parent. I bet you didn't need a class to tell you that! But, what does that actually mean? Becoming and being a parent isn't just about the 9 months of gestation. It's all that happens after that!

Who are you as a parent? What is your primary parenting style? What is your child's temperament? What does your child need to be healthy and well adjusted? How do you show love yet also set limits? What are your rights and responsibilities as a parent? How do you handle the stress of parenting? How do you deal with parenting mistakes? How do you help your children deal with divorce? How do you handle a difficult co-parenting situation? These are some of the topics we will explore throughout this class to provide you with tools for better parenting.

As a parent, you have been given the responsibility, privilege and at times daunting task of raising your child to become a healthy, responsible, independent and caring adult. Not only are you shaping who they are and will become, you are also preparing them for life without you. And through your parenting you have the opportunity to help make a better society.

I have only one guarantee for you. You will never, ever, regret being the best parent you can be. As a parent you hold the key to your child's future. Parenting well provides benefits to your child and to your own personal growth that should never be underestimated.

Parenting well provides you the opportunity to grow to become the person you are meant to be. You will never be the same after you have been a parent. Giving of the self sacrificially to another makes us better people. As you parent, you will mature in ways that no graduate program or self-help class could ever teach you.

The word "parent" may conjure up varied feelings and expectations. This may be due to the role your parents have played in your own development, your general outlook on life and your own parenting style. Understanding what you think about being a parent is critical because what you think about parenting will be displayed in your own parenting.

Let's begin by what you think about being a parent. Write your definition of what you think a parent is or should be.

_____
_____
_____
_____
_____

Our parents or caregivers have tremendous influence in how we view ourselves, others, our world, our purpose in it, and even our spiritual

"The toughest job in the world isn't being president. It's being a parent."
Coalition for America's Children Public Service Announcement

beliefs. For some of us our parents provided us with the love, guidance, and discipline we needed to become self-assured, caring and responsible adults capable of forming healthy personal relationships and continuing to mature as adults. For others, sometimes circumstances beyond our parent's control created a difficult situation for us as children due to factors such as illness, tragedy and unforeseen hardships. And then there are parents who were not equipped to parent well and although they tried, we may have been left feeling poorly equipped for the adult world. And sadly, there are parents who, due to many factors including substance abuse, mental illness, their own difficult or abusive childhoods or immaturity, created a very unhealthy place for us as children to develop.

How would you describe the parenting you received as a child?

_____

_____

_____

_____

Because of some of our backgrounds, we may need to learn new parenting skills. For others, we may simply need support to parent well, despite challenging situations we may be facing.

Full of useful and helpful insights gleaned from research, education, professional experience and hard earned wisdom as parents, this parenting program is designed to be a toolbox for parents. Some tools may be more pertinent to you in the particular stage of your parenting and personal development. Other tools may be a review and reinforcement of skills you have already integrated into your parenting. And some topics may be new to you. Like a toolbox, this is only a basic set of implements; take what you need, what might be helpful and what feels right for you and your child. Please keep in mind that your unique situation may require additional resources and assistance.

Every loving parent has had moments and days when they feel frustrated, overwhelmed, and discouraged. At times, you will lose your enthusiasm for parenting. No matter how much effort you expend being the best parent you can be, there may still be times when you do not feel like you are a good enough parent or raising a good enough child. Remember that you are doing the hardest and most important job in the world! It is no wonder that it can feel overwhelming at times. It is normal to feel like throwing in the towel at times, but never, ever give up. Just find the right tools!

This class meets you wherever you are as a parent. Whether you are parenting with a partner or as a single parent, all of us can improve ourselves, can parent more deliberately and appreciate anew how important our role truly is in our children's lives. The purpose of this class is to *educate, equip and empower you as parents as you expand your awareness of the responsibility and privilege of parenting.*

The Cost of Poor Parenting

People often ask what is wrong with poor parenting and co-parenting, if it gets the results I am looking for?

The answer is that even though you can sometimes get your children to do things you want, the cost is so high that it isn't worth it!

What are some of the costs of poor parenting and co-parenting? Costs can be:
- Financial
- Emotional
- Resentments in your children
- Resentments in your partner or ex-partner
- Children who model bad behavior and have lowered self-esteem
- Costs to your self-esteem or loss of esteem in the eyes of others

As you think back, has your lack of good parenting cost you things in the past? Was it worth it? What has it cost your children?

_____

_____

It is so important to parent well- the costs are far too great for you and your children if you don't. Jacqueline Kennedy Onassis states it simply, "If you bungle raising your children, I don't think whatever else you do well matters very much."

Past History of Parenting

We find that some of our parenting class participants grew up in homes where their parents modeled poor parenting skills. It comes as no surprise that the type of parent you become is often similar to the parenting style you grew up with. But, what if you didn't receive the kind of parenting that you needed? Or, what if you suffered maltreatment? Does this mean you are destined to be a carbon copy of them? Of course not. You can change and become a better parent by *acknowledging areas that need improvement and then learning new skills.*

In what areas of your parenting do you need improvement?

_____

_____

For example, think about your family of origin and what you learned as a child about how to communicate and how to deal (or not deal) with difficult feelings. Then, think about your own history of how you communicate and handle painful feelings. What similarities do you notice between how you parent and how you were parented?

_____

_____

_____

Do you fight or argue a lot? Do you tend to have many conflicts with your children, spouse, or ex-partner?

_____

_____

_____

We often parent in a "default setting" of how we were raised. For some of us, this may be a good thing, but for many others of us, however, some of the parenting we received left us with poor coping skills and unmet needs. Our pasts can play such a powerful role in who we are, but it is not our destiny. Learning new skills and forgiving our parents can help us to be better parents to our own children. Peter Krause reminds of this, "Parenthood …it's about guiding the next generation, and forgiving the last."

What is something you have or may need to forgive your parents for?

_____

_____

_____

The good news is that even if we didn't have the ideal parents, we can improve our own parenting skills. No matter what our parents or caregivers may have done or not done right in parenting us, and how our ex-partner is behaving, it is up to *us* to take responsibility for how we parent. "You didn't have a choice about the parents you inherited, but you do have a choice about the kind of parent you will be" (Edelman, 1992, p. 71).

What is something in your parenting that you have done (or are doing) differently that your parents did?

_____

_____

_____

Taking Responsibility

It is common for parenting and co-parenting class students to sometimes see their poor parenting as the fault of other people or situations. We hear things such as:

- I wouldn't have gotten so upset if s/he (my ex-husband/wife) wouldn't have been so late.
- I only got mad because he didn't listen to me.
- My child disrespected me so I "went off" on him.
- I told my teen how to do it five times and she still did it wrong.

Is it true that these events would trigger poor parenting skills in most people? The answer is...YES. But, it is important to understand that there is no end of events or people that have the potential to trigger poor parenting behavior or excuses in us.

We can't control all these "triggers" but we can control how we respond. And we can control how we deal with or express ourselves to our children and others.

Think back to a time when you didn't parent so well. Were you able to take some responsibility for your lack of good parenting or did you see it entirely as the fault of the other (child, partner/ex-partner)? Explain.

_____

_____

_____

No matter how challenging your past has been, either as a child, adult or as a parent, being a successful parent is within any motivated parent's reach.

Reflections on Successful Parenting:
Komen and Myers summarize some keys to successful parenting (2000, pp. 416-419).

- **Trust yourself**
You know a lot more than you think you do about parenting! "Your judgment is basically good. You have a fundamental desire to be a good parent." Also, "you know yourself and your child better than anyone else."
- **Accept your own imperfections**
You will never be a perfect parent because they don't exist! "Mistakes go with the turf. In fact, mistakes are a necessary part of the process". Sometimes that is the way we learn. "Fortunately, children are flexible creatures- durable, resilient and forgiving. Do the best you can, keep learning, and accept your kids' own imperfections in turn."
- **Ask for help when necessary**
Smart people get help when they need it, and like the song says, at times, we all need somebody to lean on. "Precisely because parenthood is so demanding, difficult and protracted, you can benefit from others' experience and wisdom."
- **Accept your child as unique**
Appreciate that there has never been or will there ever be a child just like yours. "Because every human being is one-of-a kind, your child will have individual needs, interests, capabilities, tastes and shortcomings that influence his development." And parents come with their own histories, experiences, strengths and weaknesses. "The combination of the child's individuality and the parent's individuality results in a complex,

unpredictable interaction." Don't let your own expectations dictate your child's life -discover who he is and guide him to be all that he can be.

• **Expect to be changed**

You will never be the same after you have been a parent. "Most parents end up better and more substantial human beings as a result of raising children. "By being a parent, you'll probably learn as much about yourself as you learn about your child. Parents and children inspire, guide, and teach one another."

• **Savor the moment**

"Value what you have. Experience every aspect of parenthood as fully as possible." You only have today. Remember that.

Of the reflections, above, which ones are you practicing?

_____
_____
_____

Which ones would you like to?

_____
_____
_____

Parenting Basics—Things you should know

> *"Life affords no greater responsibility, no greater privilege, than the raising of the next generation."*
> C. Everett Koop, MD

Parent's Rights and Responsibilities

Being a parent is such an integral and vital part of our society that our legal system has enacted laws to protect our rights as parents from undue governmental interference and also to protect children from parental abuse and neglect. The rights pertaining to the care and custody of our children are actually fundamental rights guaranteed by the United States Constitution and cannot be interfered with except to protect a child. Even where the government intervenes to protect children and removes them from the home of a parent, the goal of the court is to reunify children with their families whenever possible.

What exactly are your rights and responsibilities as parents? California law provides parameters for understanding what these are. The following section from *Kids and the Law* includes some of your rights and responsibilities (State Bar of California and The California Bar Foundation, 2010, pp. 10-11).

Custody and Control: "Parents must make important decisions about their children's lives, such as where the children will live, what school they will attend, when medical care is appropriate and what if any religion they will practice. These rights are constitutionally protected and generally cannot be taken away unless it can be shown that the parents are unfit."

Cooperation and Obedience: "Parents are expected to control their children and are permitted to discipline them (not to the point of abuse or neglect, however)."

Parental Responsibilities: Parents must support their children. "They are legally obligated to provide their children with the necessities of life. Such necessities are not limited to food, clothing, and shelter but also include medical care. This responsibility falls on both of the parents."

Supervision and Control of Children: "Parents may be morally responsible for supervising and controlling their child. However, parents are generally not legally responsible for the acts of their children. There are exceptions. For example, parents who encourage their children to break the law may be found guilty of contributing to the delinquency of a minor. Also, parents who know or should have known that their child engages in improper conduct, or who aid or encourages such conduct, may be held liable for their children's acts."

What is Child Abuse and Neglect (maltreatment)?

You may be wondering why it is important to understand this difficult topic. Well, first of all, because it is your duty to protect your children from all forms of child abuse and neglect (maltreatment). Secondly, you may not know exactly what constitutes child abuse or neglect. Some parenting practices that are considered maltreatment in California today you may have experienced as a child, learned from previous generations or practiced yourself. And in some cultures some of the following may be considered acceptable parenting or discipline techniques, but are considered child abuse and/or neglect and are not allowed in this state.

According to the Center for Disease Control (Child Maltreatment Prevention, 2013) "child maltreatment includes all types of abuse and neglect of a child under the age of 18 by a parent, caregiver, or another person in a custodial role (e.g., clergy, coach, teacher). There are four common types of abuse":

- Physical Abuse
- Sexual Abuse
- Emotional Abuse
- Neglect

Though "there are several types of child abuse, the core element that ties them together is the emotional effect on the child. Children need predictability, structure, clear boundaries, and the knowledge that their parents are looking out for their safety. Abused children cannot predict how their parents will act. Their world is an unpredictable, frightening place with no rules. Whether the abuse is a slap, a harsh comment, stony silence, or not knowing if there will be dinner on the table tonight, the end result is a child that feels unsafe, uncared for, and alone" (Smith, M. and Segal, J., 2013, p. 2).

What Are the Major Types of Child Abuse and Neglect?
(Child Welfare Information Gateway, 2011, California: Child Abuse and Neglect)

Physical Abuse: Citation: Welf. & Inst. Code § 300
A child may be considered dependent when:

> • The child has suffered, or there is a substantial risk that the child will suffer, serious physical harm inflicted nonaccidentally upon the child by the child's parent or guardian. For the purposes of this subdivision, a court may find there is a substantial risk of serious future injury based on the manner in which a less serious injury was inflicted, a history of repeated inflictions of injuries on the child or the child's siblings, or a combination of these and other actions by the parent or guardian that indicate the child is at risk of serious physical harm.

• The child is younger than age 5 and has suffered severe physical abuse by a parent or by any person known by the parent, if the parent knew or reasonably should have known that the person was physically abusing the child.
• The child's parent or guardian caused the death of another child through abuse or neglect.
• The child has been subjected to an act or acts of cruelty by the parent or guardian or a member of his or her household, or the parent or guardian has failed to adequately protect the child from an act or acts of cruelty when the parent or guardian knew or reasonably should have known that the child was in danger of being subjected to an act or acts of cruelty.

• **For the purposes of this subdivision, 'severe physical abuse' means:**

   • Any single act of abuse that causes physical trauma of sufficient severity that, if left untreated, would cause permanent physical disfigurement, permanent physical disability, or death
   • Any single act of sexual abuse that causes significant bleeding, deep bruising, or significant external or internal swelling
   • More than one act of physical abuse, each of which causes bleeding, deep bruising, significant external or internal swelling, bone fracture, or unconsciousness
   • The willful, prolonged failure to provide adequate food

Neglect: Citation: Welf. & Inst. Code § 300

A child may be considered dependent when:

• The child has suffered, or there is a substantial risk that the child will suffer, serious physical harm or illness as a result of:

   • The failure or inability of the parent or guardian to adequately supervise or protect the child
   • The willful or negligent failure of the parent or guardian to adequately supervise or protect the child from the conduct of the custodian with whom the child has been left
   • The willful or negligent failure of the parent or guardian to provide the child with adequate food, clothing, shelter, or medical treatment
   • The inability of the parent or guardian to provide regular care for the child due to the parent's or guardian's mental illness, developmental disability, or substance abuse
   • The child's sibling has been abused or neglected, and there is a substantial risk that the child will be abused or neglected. The court shall consider the circumstances surrounding the abuse or neglect of the sibling, the age and gender of each child, the nature of the abuse or neglect of the sibling, the mental condition of the parent or guardian, and any other factors the court considers probative in determining whether there

is a substantial risk to the child.

Sexual Abuse/Exploitation: Citation: Welf. & Inst. Code § 300; Penal Code § 11165.1

A child is considered dependent if he or she has been sexually abused, there is a substantial risk that the child will be sexually abused, as defined in § 11165.1 of the Penal Code, by his or her parent, guardian, or a household member; or the parent or guardian has failed to adequately protect the child from sexual abuse when the parent or guardian knew or reasonably should have known that the child was in danger of sexual abuse.

'Sexual abuse' means sexual assault or sexual exploitation as defined below:

'Sexual assault' includes rape, incest, sodomy, lewd or lascivious acts upon a child, or child molestation. 'Sexual exploitation' refers to any of the following:

> • Depicting a minor engaged in obscene acts; preparing, selling, or distributing obscene matter that depicts minors; employing a minor to perform obscene acts
> • Knowingly permitting or encouraging a child to engage in, or assisting others to engage in, prostitution or a live performance involving obscene sexual conduct, or to either pose or model alone or with others for purposes of preparing a film, photograph, negative, slide, drawing, painting, or other pictorial depiction involving obscene sexual conduct
> • Depicting a child in, or knowingly developing, duplicating, printing, or exchanging any film, photograph, videotape, negative, or slide in which a child is engaged in an act of obscene sexual conduct

Emotional Abuse: Citation: Welf. & Inst. Code § 300

A child is considered dependent if he or she is suffering serious emotional damage, or is at substantial risk of suffering serious emotional damage, as evidenced by severe anxiety, depression, withdrawal, or untoward aggressive behavior toward self or others, as a result of the conduct of the parent or guardian, or who has no parent or guardian capable of providing appropriate care. No child shall be found to be a dependent person if the willful failure of the parent or guardian to provide adequate mental health treatment is based on a sincerely held religious belief and if a less intrusive judicial intervention is available.

[Examples of emotional child abuse include:

> • Constant belittling, shaming, and humiliating a child.
> • Calling names and making negative comparisons to others.

• Telling a child he or she is "no good," "worthless," "bad," or "a mistake."
• Frequent yelling, threatening, or bullying.
• Ignoring or rejecting a child as punishment, giving him or her the silent treatment.
• Limited physical contact with the child—no hugs, kisses, or other signs of affection.
• Exposing the child to violence or the abuse of others, whether it be the abuse of a parent, a sibling, or even a pet" (Smith, M. and Segal, J., 2013, p. 2).]

Abandonment: Citation: Welf. & Inst. Code § 300

A child is considered dependent when:

• The child has been left without any provision for support.
• Physical custody of the child has been voluntarily surrendered pursuant to § 1255.7 of the Health and Safety Code, and the child has not been reclaimed within the 14-day period specified in subdivision (e) of that section.
• The child's parent has been incarcerated or institutionalized and cannot arrange for the care of the child.
• A relative or other adult custodian with whom the child resides or has been left is unwilling or unable to provide care or support for the child, the whereabouts of the parent are unknown, and reasonable efforts to locate the parent have been unsuccessful.
• The child has been freed for adoption by one or both parents for 12 months by either relinquishment or termination of parental rights or an adoption petition has not been granted.

Persons Responsible for the Child: Citation: Welf. & Inst. Code § 300

A person responsible for a child's welfare includes the child's parent or guardian. As used in this section, 'guardian' means the legal guardian of the child.

Exceptions: Citation: Welf. & Inst. Code §§ 300; 300.5

Serious physical harm does not include reasonable and age-appropriate spanking to the buttocks where there is no evidence of serious physical injury.

No child shall be found to be dependent solely due to the lack of an emergency shelter for the family.

A physical disability, such as blindness or deafness, is not considered a bar to raising happy and well-adjusted children unless a parent's disability prevents him or her from exercising care and control.

A child whose parent has been adjudged a dependent child shall not be considered to be at risk of abuse or neglect solely because of the age, dependent status, or foster care status of the parent.

In any case in which a child is alleged to be dependent on the basis that he or she is in need of medical care, the court, in making that finding, shall give consideration to any treatment being provided to the child by spiritual means through prayer alone in accordance with the tenets and practices of a recognized church or religious denomination by an accredited practitioner thereof.

In your own words, and using the statutes above, how would you explain the following?

Physical abuse:

_____
_____
_____

Neglect:

_____
_____
_____

Sexual abuse/exploitation:

_____
_____
_____

Emotional Abuse:

_____
_____
_____

Abandonment:

_____
_____
_____

What is the exception related to spanking?

_____
_____
_____

As a parent it is your duty to not only care for your child but also to protect him from all forms of maltreatment. Child abuse and neglect can have profound, devastating, and long-lasting effects on children, and also throughout their entire lives. "A child who is maltreated is likely to develop a sense of powerlessness, leading to negative and often harmful adaptations, such as delinquency and adult criminality"… and is "more likely to suffer from serious health issues, such as increased risk for smoking, alcoholism, substance abuse, eating disorders, obesity, depression, suicide, and other problems" (Regoli, Hewitt and Delisi, 2010, p. 376).

Although child abuse and neglect can and does occur intentionally, it can also occur when parents find themselves poorly equipped to parent well. The U.S. Department of Health and Human Services Child Welfare Information Gateway explains that "the ability of a parent to provide adequate care for a child depends partly on his/her emotional maturity, coping skills, knowledge about children, mental capacity, and parenting skills" (1993).

Sometimes, if we had childhood histories of abuse or neglect, we may not know any other way to parent, and may not be aware that our behavior has crossed the line into abuse. Smith and Segal help us to understand this and provide guidelines for identifying if and when we are being abusive or neglectful in our parenting.

> Raising children is one of life's greatest challenges and can trigger anger and frustration in the most even tempered. If you grew up in a household where screaming and shouting or violence was the norm, you may not know any other way to raise your kids.
>
> Recognizing that you have a problem is the biggest step to getting help. If you yourself were raised in an abusive situation, that can be extremely difficult. Children experience their world as normal. It may have been normal in your family to be slapped or pushed for little to no reason, or that mother was too drunk to cook dinner. It may have been normal for your parents to call you stupid, clumsy, or worthless. Or it may have been normal to watch your mother get beaten up by your father.
>
> It is only as adults that we have the perspective to step back and take a hard look at what is normal and what is abusive. The following is a list of warning signs that you may be crossing the line into abuse:

How do you know when you've crossed the line?

> • **You can't stop the anger.** What starts as a swat on the backside may turn into multiple hits getting harder and harder. You may shake your child harder and harder and finally throw him or her down. You find yourself screaming louder and louder and can't stop yourself.
> • **You feel emotionally disconnected from your child.** You may feel so overwhelmed that you don't want anything to do with your child. Day after day, you just want to be left alone and for your child to be quiet.
> • **Meeting the daily needs of your child seems impossible.**

While everyone struggles with balancing dressing, feeding, and getting kids to school or other activities, if you continually can't manage to do it, it's a sign that something might be wrong.
• **Other people have expressed concern.** It may be easy to bristle at other people expressing concern. However, consider carefully what they have to say. Are the words coming from someone you normally respect and trust? Denial is not an uncommon reaction. (Smith, M. and Segal, J. 2013, p. 5)

Parents that feel overwhelmed with their life situations in combination with the stresses of parenting, often react poorly to their children and may harm them. Harming children is indefensible, no matter your situation or your child's behavior. Remember, "children are never to blame for the harm others do to them" (Centers for Disease Control, 2012, Who is at risk for child maltreatment?). Children are vulnerable and should always be protected from any form of maltreatment. If you find you are struggling and unable to cope with a challenging child or difficult situation, or have crossed the line into abusive or neglectful behavior toward your child, get help. You will find there are many resources and services to support you and your children. (See Resources)

Understanding factors that place your child at risk for maltreatment and those that protect him can also help you determine if you and your child may need extra help. The Centers for Disease Control and Prevention (Child Maltreatment: Risk and Protective Factors, 2012) identifies risk factors that combine to place a child at risk of maltreatment and protective factors that provide a buffer against those risks.

Child Maltreatment: Risk and Protective Factors

Risk Factors for Child Maltreatment

A combination of individual, relational, community and societal factors contribute to the risk of child maltreatment. Although children are not responsible for the harm inflicted upon them, certain characteristics have been found to increase their risk of being maltreated. Risk factors are those characteristics associated with child maltreatment—they may or may not be direct causes.

Individual Risk Factors for Victimization Include:
  • Children younger than 4 years of age
  • Special needs that may increase caregiver burden (e.g., disabilities, mental retardation, mental health issues, and chronic physical illnesses)

Risk Factors for Perpetration

Individual Risk Factors

   • Parents' lack of understanding of children's needs, child development and parenting skills

- Parents' history of child maltreatment in family of origin
- Substance abuse and/or mental health issues including depression in the family
- Parental characteristics such as young age, low education, single parenthood, large number of dependent children, and low income
- Nonbiological, transient caregivers in the home (e.g., mother's male partner)
- Parental thoughts and emotions that tend to support or justify maltreatment behaviors

Family Risk Factors

- Social isolation
- Family disorganization, dissolution, and violence, including intimate partner violence
- Parenting stress, poor parent-child relationships, and negative interactions

[Parenting stress can result from a family history of violence, drug or alcohol abuse, poverty and chronic health problems and insufficient social support (Centers for Disease Control, 2012, Understanding Child Maltreatment).]

Community Risk Factors

- Community violence
- Concentrated neighborhood disadvantage (e.g., high poverty and residential instability, high unemployment rates, and high density of alcohol outlets), and poor social connections.

What risk factors, if any, is your child currently experiencing?

_____

How are you protecting your child from those risk factors?

_____

As a parent, family or in your community, what risk factors are you experiencing?

_____

What are you doing to address or buffer against those?

_____

Protective Factors for Child Maltreatment

Protective factors may buffer children from the effects of the risk factors associated with abuse or neglect. These factors exist at various levels. Protective factors have not been studied as extensively or rigorously as risk factors. However, identifying and understanding protective factors are equally as important as researching risk factors. There is scientific evidence to support the following protective factor:

Family Protective Factors

• Supportive family environment and social networks

Several other potential protective factors have been identified. Research is ongoing to determine whether the following factors do indeed buffer children from the effects of maltreatment.

Family Protective Factors

• Nurturing parenting skills
• Stable family relationships
• Household rules and child monitoring
• Parental employment
• Adequate housing
• Access to health care and social services
• Caring adults outside the family who can serve as role models or mentors

Community Protective Factors

• Communities that support parents and take responsibility for preventing abuse

Of the protective factors, above, which ones are currently a part of your family life?

_____
_____

Source: Centers for Disease Control and Prevention, Child Maltreatment: Risk and Protective Factors (Atlanta: National Center for Injury Prevention and Control, 2012)

Common Parenting Mistakes

Sometimes, well-meaning parents act poorly towards their children, not because they do not love their children but because they have too much stress (See Ch. 8) in their lives and/or because they lack the parenting skills or knowledge to deal with common parenting challenges. Expert pediatrician and author Vincent Iannelli, M.D, outlines seven common mistakes that parents make, that if not addressed, can lead to much frustration, strained relationships with your child, ineffective and poor parenting.

Parents don't usually start out wanting to make mistakes. Too often though, they only rely on their 'parenting instincts' and don't try to get help with common parenting issues and problems. Unfortunately, many of us aren't instinctively able to know what to do in each and every situation that we face as parents, and we can make mistakes from time to time.

Learning to overcome these 7 common parenting mistakes will get you a long way towards being a more effective parent:

1) Not Trying To Fix Problems

Either because they think that certain problems can't be fixed or they simply are quick to accept them, many parents endure months or years of frustration living with common problems. This might include bedtime battles, frequent night awakenings, or frequent temper tantrums and behavior problems in older children.

Although it may take some hard work, most problems that you face as a parent can be worked through and changed or fixed. You may need some help, though. Your baby may not have come with instructions, but there are plenty of books, websites, and people, that can help guide you through the challenges of parenting. Your pediatrician and other health professionals can also be helpful when facing more difficult or persistent problems.

2) Overestimating or Underestimating Problems

Before you try to fix problems, you have to first decide what is and isn't a problem. And if it is a problem, how big of a problem are you facing.

Is it a big problem if your:

> • preschooler has occasional tantrums?
> • 5 or 6 year old is 'caught' playing doctor?
> • teen begins to test his limits, spends more time away from his family, or tries to be more independent?

In general, the answer in all three situations is no. These are simple age appropriate issues that should be expected. On the other hand, you shouldn't take lightly a problem like a teen caught smoking, stealing, or cheating.

3) Having Unrealistic Expectations

If you have unrealistic expectations of what your kids should be doing, you can actually create problems. This often happens when parents get frustrated or impatient with a 2 1/2 year old who still isn't interested in potty training, a 6 year old who is wetting the bed, or a moody teenager. So make sure that your expectations match what your kids are developmentally able or expected to be doing.

4) Being Inconsistent

Few things can harm your children more than an inconsistent parenting style. If you are sometimes very strict, but give in other times or simply don't seem to care what your kids are doing, they will have a very hard time knowing what is expected of them and how to act.

5) Not Having Rules or Setting Limits

You may think that you are doing your kids a favor by letting them do whatever they want, but younger children find it especially hard to live without any limits. Having rules, setting limits, consistent routines, and offering limited choices will help your child know and expect what is coming throughout the day.

6) Fighting Back

In the book, Setting Limits with your Strong- Willed Child, Dr. Robert MacKenzie describes fighting back as the 'family dance,' in which you can become 'stuck in these destructive patterns of communication.' We aren't talking about physically fighting with your child, but fighting back can take other forms, like getting mad, yelling, and repeating yourself over and over.

Fighting or arguing with your kids offers them negative attention and a lot of power over you, since they are able to trigger such strong reactions. Instead of stopping problem behaviors, fighting back will lead you to 'unintentionally rewarding the misbehavior you're trying to stop.'

Instead of fighting back, you can do better by stopping power struggles and learning more effective discipline techniques, like time-out and using logical and natural consequences, and not taking a lot of time fighting before you use them.

7) Not Changing What Doesn't Work

Not recognizing or changing your parenting techniques that aren't working is almost as big a problem as not trying to fix problems in the first place. Is what you are doing working? For instance, you may think that spanking is an effective form of discipline, but if you have to use it each day to correct the same problem or behavior, then it should be obvious that it isn't. Or if your bedtime routine involves your child repeatedly getting up and out of bed, stretches out to an hour, and leaves you frustrated and your child tired the next morning, then you likely need a new way to help your child go to bed.

What mistakes have you seen in yourself or are you currently struggling with?

_____
_____
_____

Is there something you could do to improve that area of your parenting?

_____
_____
_____

Understanding Your Child

> *"The child must know that he is a miracle, that since the beginning of the world there hasn't been, and until the end of the world there will not be, another child like him."*
> Pablo Casals

Your child is a gift. Helping to discover your child's unique giftedness is a parent's awesome privilege. Your child largely learns about who he is, his value, and how he fits in the world through you. At times this is easy. When you hold your healthy newborn, watch your contented sleeping toddler or take your child to the zoo for the first time, your child may seem to be such a wonder. Other times you may need to work a bit harder to appreciate their giftedness! In order to do this, it is important not to compare your child with any other child, even your other children. Although this may be a natural tendency and not always harmful, if you find yourself being overly critical and judgmental of your child you may be holding your child to a standard that is not fair or reasonable.

Your Child's Developmental Stage

Learn what developmental stage your child is in. Your child is constantly growing and changing. "Developmental stages" help us to understand this process and provides a framework with milestones to help us assess our child's growth and development. Although we can easily see the physical development of our children, it is critical to understand that our children are also growing in other areas as well, including emotionally, cognitively, and socially.

According to psychologist Erik Ericson, the socialization process consists of eight stages. (See chart.) This social and emotional development starts in infancy and continues into adulthood. Each stage is regarded as a psychosocial crisis which arises and demands resolution before the next stage can be satisfactorily negotiated. Understanding the stage your child is in and what he needs to successfully move to the next stage is important so that can you can provide the necessary support for that growth to occur. (See Resources for additional information concerning these stages.)

Stage	Basic Conflict	Important Events	Outcome
Infancy (birth to 18 months)	Trust vs. Mistrust	Feeding	Children develop a sense of trust when caregivers provide reliabilty, care, and affection. A lack of this will lead to mistrust.
Early Childhood (2 to 3 years)	Autonomy vs. Shame and Doubt	Toilet Training	Children need to develop a sense of personal control over physical skills and a sense of independence. Success leads to feelings of autonomy, failure results in feelings of shame and doubt.
Preschool (3 to 5 years)	Initiative vs. Guilt	Exploration	Children need to begin asserting control and power over the environment. Success in this stage leads to a sense of purpose. Children who try to exert too much power experience disapproval, resulting in a sense of guilt.
School Age (6 to 11 years)	Industry vs. Inferiority	School	Children need to cope with new social and academic demands. Success leads to a sense of competence, while failure results in feelings of inferiority.
Adolescence (12 to 18 years)	Identity vs. Role Confusion	Social Relationships	Teens need to develop a sense of self and personal identity. Success leads to an ability to stay true to yourself, while failure leads to role confusion and a weak sense of self.
Young Adulthood (19 to 40 years)	Intimacy vs. Isolation	Relationships	Young adults need to form intimate, loving relationships with other people. Success leads to strong relationships, while failure results in loneliness and isolation.
Middle Adulthood (40 to 65 years)	Generativity vs. Stagnation	Work and Parenthood	Adults need to create or nurture things that will outlast them, often by having children or creating a positive change that benefits other people. Success leads to feelings of usefulness and accomplishment, while failure results in shallow involvement in the world.
Maturity (65 to death)	Ego Integrity vs. Despair	Reflection on Life	Older adults need to look back on life and feel a sense of fulfillment. Success at this stage leads to feelings of wisdom, while failure results in regret, bitterness, and despair.

Understanding the stage your child is in, in all areas of his development and what is considered normal is important in determining what parenting approaches are most helpful in maximizing your child's growth and potential. (It can also help you to relax and enjoy parenting more when you know what is normal infant, child or adolescent behavior.) Always keep in mind any developmental, physical, health related issue or stress your child maybe experiencing.

And, what is normal at a certain stage of development may not be so at other stages. For example, your toddler walks around everywhere with his thumb and blanket; that is normal for a two year old, but may be of concern if your eight year old is doing the same behavior.

We may not always know or be aware of all of the growth and changes that are occurring in our children or what is considered normal growth or behavior for a certain age. If you are not certain what is "normal" for your child or what developmental milestones your child should be achieving, your best resource may be your child's pediatrician, but other helpful information may be found in books, health care and

mental health professionals, parenting classes, reputable websites, your child's teacher and child development classes. (See Resources)

It is very helpful to take the time to learn about the stage your child is in and what the next stage is that he will be entering. It will help you to assist him with the transitions of moving from one stage to another and will allow you to make parenting adjustments as needed.

Your Child's Temperament/Your Temperament

What is temperament? Temperament is defined as the features of your personality that are present at birth and have a genetic and biological basis. Temperament underlies how we respond to our environment. Your temperament, or basic disposition, interacts with environmental influences to create your personality. It can be observed in infancy and remains constant throughout your life.

Learn about your child's temperament. Learn about your temperament. Learn about how the two interact. This is critically important as it can provide insight into many aspects of your child's behavior and may explain why you respond to your child the way that you do. It can help to answer why children behave differently even if they are the same age, gender, or even from the same family. Every parent and child relationship is unique and dynamic, and temperament plays a key role in that dynamic. (See Resources)

According to Mary Sheedy Kurcinka in Raising Your Spirited Child, (2006, pp. 12-15) nine characteristics make up a child's temperament. These are:

1. Intensity: the strength of a child's emotional response
2. Persistence: the ease or difficulty a child has stopping or letting go of an activity or idea that is important to her
3. Sensitivity: a child's awareness and sensitivity to tastes, textures, temperature, noise and emotions
4. Perceptiveness: a child's awareness of the colors, people, noises, and objects around her. Perceptiveness determines a child's ability to stay focused.
5. Adaptability: a child's ability to adapt to changes in her schedule or routine
6. Regularity: a child's regularity or irregularity in terms of her daily rhythms- eating, sleeping and elimination
7. Energy: a child's basic energy level-quiet and relaxed or on the move and busy
8. First Reaction: a child's level of comfort or discomfort in new situations
9. Mood: a child's tendency to be happy and content or serious and moody

Every child has different levels of each characteristic. Looking at the nine characteristics, what level (low-medium-high) does your child have for each characteristic?

- Intensity: low----med----high
- Persistence: low----med----high
- Sensitivity: low----med----high
- Perceptiveness: low----med----high
- Adaptability: low----med----high
- Regularity: low----med----high
- Energy: low----med----high
- First Reaction: low----med----high
- Mood: low----med----high

Identifying your child's temperamental traits is like taking an X-ray. It helps you to recognize what's going on inside your child so you can understand how he is reacting to the world around him and why. Once you realize the reasons behind his responses, you can learn to work with them, ease the hassles, teach new behaviors where they are needed, and, most importantly, help your child understand and like himself (Kurcinka, 2006, p. 40).

Your children are constantly "telling" you who they are. One of our tasks as parents is to first discover their temperament, cherish it, understand its strengths and weaknesses, and help our children to understand themselves.

What are your children "telling" you about who they are?

_____
_____
_____

A child's temperament may be easy or hard for you based on the "match" between you and your child's temperament. Having a child with a very different temperament or very similar temperament can lead to significant challenges. Every temperament has its strengths and weaknesses. Learn to delight in the different, positive traits of your child, nurture those strengths, and help them to understand and work on the weaknesses posed by their natural temperament.

What are some of the strengths of your child's temperament?

_____
_____
_____

What are some areas that need strengthening?

_____
_____
_____

Your Child with Special Needs

According to the U.S Department of Education, one of every 10 children under the age of 14 has some type of special need. This can include any physical, cognitive, or medical disability, or chronic or life threatening illness. Although children with special needs often require much more from parents and support systems, a loving parent who is informed and engaged is every child's best resource. (Editorial Projects in Education Research Center, 2011)

Below are a few tips for parents of children who have a disability:
- Learn as much as you can about your child's disability.
- Find programs to help your child.
- Talk to other parents of children with disabilities.
- Join a support group.
- Stick to a daily routine.
- Take it one day at a time.
- Take good care of yourself.

(Illnesses and Disabilities, 2009)

From the tips listed above, which ones are you actively doing?

_____

_____

_____

Which ones pose more of challenge for you?

_____

_____

_____

Your Child in Your Family

Learn about who your child is in *your* family. Whether you have one, two or several children will have a significant impact on every member of the family. Your child's birth order affects how he learns and perceives reality.

"Birth order is designed to give you clues about what an individual is like and what their thoughts processes and feelings are" (Leman, 2009, p. 72). Life from a first born's vantage point versus a middle child's or the youngest will create different experiences within the same family just because of the birth order.

There are also certain personality traits that are often identified with a child's birth order. For example, first born children are often achievers and tend to be perfectionists. They have only adult role models to learn from, mom and dad, or other parent figures. Middle children, on the other hand, tend to be mediators but also know how to fend for themselves. The youngest child in the family may be outgoing, personable, and manipulative. Have you noticed some of these traits in your children? Which ones?

_____

_____

_____

The most important thing to remember, no matter the birth order of your children is to make *each child feel loved and valued.* Being aware of the role of birth order on your child's experience in your family may provide you with additional insight and empathy for your child.

Your Child as a Sibling- Dealing with Sibling Rivalry

According to the American Academy of Pediatrics, (Dealing with Sibling Rivalry, 2004),

> Nearly every parent with more than one child has experienced the frustration of sibling rivalry. Despite the best attempts at keeping harmony in the family, brothers and sisters will fight over toys, tattle on one another, argue, tease, criticize, or become physically aggressive, leading parents to ask themselves: "What have I done wrong? Why can't our household be peaceful?"
>
> As annoying and upsetting as this rivalry can be, much of it is quite normal. Some jealousy and friction between siblings is a part of growing up, although it is worse in some families than in others.
>
> Why does rivalry among your children occur? In part, it is a competition for your attention and love. You are very important in their lives, and they would rather not share you with anyone, particularly a brother or sister. That in itself is enough to cause dissension. Other factors contribute to this rivalry as well, including the personalities of your children, their mutual or differing interests, their ages, the amount of time they spend with one another and with you, and even the favoritism you may show toward one child, however unintentional. With so many factors at play, some squabbling is inevitable.

Guidelines for Parental Management of Sibling Rivalry

- Be fair.
- Avoid making comparisons between your children.
- Encourage the children to work out their own differences.
- Avoid taking sides on sibling conflicts. Be impartial, and do not show a preference for one child or another.
- Set guidelines on how children can disagree and resolve conflicts.
- Discourage tattling.

• When it is necessary to punish or reprimand, do it with the child alone in a quiet, private place.
• Use regular family meetings for all family members to express their thoughts and feelings, as well as to plan the week's events and to give positive recognition and rewards (allowance, special privileges).

Which of the guidelines, above, do you use with your children?

_____

_____

_____

The key to managing sibling rivalry depends on how the family reacts to the natural competition for a family's limited resources of time, love, attention, etc. Sibling rivalry can play a significant role in how a child views himself as a person, within the family, at school, later in life and can even determine their role in life. Children who feel they are not getting a fair amount of time and attention may fight to be heard and crave validation all their life, because they did not get it at home. In addition, if children feel they are not heard or are displaced, more rivalry will occur.

Is there ever a time when parents should intervene in sibling rivalry? When is it simply a normal spat and when is it potentially a more serious problem? What can parents do to keep the peace? (Amitay, 2012)

There are times when parents need to intervene in sibling conflicts. Signs include:

• Conflicts are more prevalent
• The child, on the losing end, is changing their demeanor, mood or behavior, or it's having an impact at school
• If the stronger, bigger or older sibling is always winning the rivalry, "teaching" the younger, smaller or weaker one that might makes right

For conflicts that need parental intervention, parents can:

• Help children to negotiate
• Make sure both children's needs are being heard and respected by the other child
• Accept that you cannot treat all your kids equally all the time. Children are not equal, especially with age differences. Older children might have more responsibilities because they can handle them and get more rights than the younger child, so parents have to take that into consideration. Parents also need to take into consideration a child's temperament, personality, needs and the actual dynamics of the situation. And regardless of age and gender, ask yourself these questions, as a parent:

* Does one of the children feel that they are not getting as much attention, respect or not having their needs met?
* Does one of children feel that something is unfair to them? Children are going to feel that things are unfair all the time, so an unempathic parent says, "Too bad." A parent with more empathy explains why the other child is being treated differently, and tries to compensate in some way, so the child does not feel they are always getting less than their sibling.

• Most importantly, as a parent, be responsive to each child's needs and when the, "It's not fair", is a valid point your child is making, try to compensate in a big or small way.

Your Child Outside of Your Family

Learn about your child's role in society. Your child's gender, cultural identity, religious beliefs and any special needs play significant roles in his experience, in not only your family, but in the larger context of his school and community. (Blended families, step- and half- siblings also significantly affect your child.) Each of these will have an impact on your child and is important in understanding each individual child.

Learn about your child's rights. Just as you have many rights and responsibilities as parents, so too your children have legal rights. Children have the right to food, clothing, shelter, medical care and an education. They also have the right to not be abused or neglected. Everything else you give or do not give your child is up pretty much up to you.

Your Adolescent: Appreciating the Task of Adolescence

"Your defining act of love for your child will not be the 2:00 A.M. feeding, the sleepless, fretful night beside him in the hospital, or the second job you took to pay for college. Your zenith will occur in the face of a withering blast of frightening rage from your adolescent, in allowing no rage from yourself in response. Your finest moment may well be your darkest. And you will be a parent" (Bradley, 2002, p. xvii).

The adolescent years are a time of great change for both you and your teen. Adolescence (early teens to mid-twenties) is a time for your child to explore and establish his identity, to gain a separate sense of self apart from you, to learn about the consequences of good and bad decisions, and to explore their own values and beliefs. It is also a time when their peer group influences greatly increases. The difficult part for us as parents is to understand that while this may drive us crazy and be frightening, many of the behaviors of adolescents are actually developmentally *necessary to help them develop their own identity, appreciate the consequences of their choices more fully, and prepare them for adult life.*

One of the most important things your adolescent must accomplish during this period is forming their identity. According to psychologist Eric Erickson, in order for an adolescent to achieve their own personal identity he must have worked through four prior stages successfully. The prior stages (trust versus mistrust, autonomy versus shame, initiative verses guilt, and industry versus inferiority) successfully negotiated, develop the qualities of trust, autonomy, initiative and industry. All these qualities are necessary in order for an adolescent to form a clear sense of identity. If an adolescent has been unable to negotiate the prior stages successfully, this may lead to maladaptive and malignant tendencies, including a sense of fear, guilt, shame, inferiority, and insecurity, which may cause great difficulty in developing a sense of true identity. (See Ch. 2 and resources for more information on these stages.)

One of your tasks as a parent of an adolescent is to create a supportive environment for your young adult to form a healthy identity and self-image. Transitioning from a dependent child to an independent, responsible young adult includes "trying out" new behaviors, versions of self, relationships, values, beliefs, and experiences. (How else do you learn about life if you don't try it out for yourself?) The hard part for us as parents is that we may not appreciate that even the most mature adolescent's transition will get "messy" at times.

What are appropriate ways that teens display their sense of separateness and independence from their parents?

_____

_____

What are some maladaptive or harmful ways that teens assert their growing autonomy and independence?

_____

_____

This time of transition includes experimenting with conduct and attitudes that are appropriate for that task, but may also include other behaviors that may be maladaptive and harmful. Discerning between the two may not always be easy. Your adolescent will no doubt try to convince you that "nothing bad will happen" and "everyone is doing it". In allowing your teen more autonomy, it is important for you to trust your "gut" and accurately gage your child's level of maturity. Remember, trust is earned. If your teen has acted responsibly, then privileges should be expanded. If, on the other hand, your child is more immature, has acted irresponsibly or is more of a follower, additional control may need to be continued or implemented.

Adolescents need to encounter life with its adversity, make mistakes and fail in order to become competent young adults who can navigate life's many challenges and learn to make wise choices. Wisdom comes from experience and experience comes from making mistakes and learning from them.

What consequences of a poor choice has your adolescent experienced that has taught him a valuable lesson?

_____

_____

Do you think explaining the lesson to your adolescent would have had as much impact as suffering the consequence of that bad decision?

The challenge for parents of teens is to know when to let our teens struggle and when to intervene. "Finding the right level of involvement in your teenager's life is one of the toughest challenges you may face as a parent" (Gottman, 1997, p. 203). Your parental instincts and your child's maturity and previous behavior are important to weigh in making these decisions. (There are some signs at the end of this section that are also helpful.) Although school, extended family and the community play a role and have an impact in our teen's life, the onus is on us, as parents, however, to guide, observe, counsel and intervene where necessary. Despite protests to the contrary, your guidance will always matter to your child. Research has borne out the critical role that parents play in an adolescent's development and decision making abilities.

As a parent, what can you do to prevent risky teen behavior? This article provides helpful tips to influence your teen's choices, values and behavior.

Preventing Risky Teen Behavior

Teenagers. For parents facing the teen years, just thinking about the word may conjure up fears and uncertainty. Some are valid; others may be overblown. Adolescence is indeed a time of great change and personal growth for a teen. Many opportunities to engage in harmful or delinquent activity also present themselves during this stage of life. Can parents do anything to minimize the likelihood that their child will become involved in risky behaviors? Absolutely!

Parenting an adolescent requires being prepared and staying informed. Resolve, self-sacrifice, flexibility and patience are vital. Parents who understand the changes that occur during adolescence, what risks their children are exposed to and what they can do to prevent risky behavior are better equipped to guide them to become healthy, caring and responsible young adults. Laguna Beach therapist, David Lindquist, MFCC, addresses how hard adolescence can be for a teen, but he also underscores the challenge of parenting one. He shares, "Being an adolescent is difficult; the only thing harder is being a responsible parent of an adolescent."

It is important to realize that no matter where your child goes to school or where you live, your child will be exposed to drugs and alcohol, along with opportunities to engage in other risky behavior. Although peers become more important at this stage in your child's life, you still hold tremendous power to influence their choices, values and behavior. Use it! Here's how:

• **Model responsible behavior.** By your actions and words you are constantly teaching your children your values and priorities. Your own habits regarding alcohol, drugs and tobacco communicate your views on those substances. At a recent conference on how to raise a drug free child, Ross. M. Brower, M.D. states "The first thing parents must do to create drug free kids is to lead by example." Children are also learning from you how to handle difficult feelings, solve problems, treat others and themselves.

• **Engage with your teen.** Your teen needs you to be involved in their lives, even if they make you feel unwelcome! Brower emphasizes the ability that parents have to impact their child's decisions. "Parents have profound power, but they need to engage." Maintain family rituals such as eating together. The presence of parents at key times during the day (morning, mealtimes, after school) reduces substance abuse, emotional distress, and delays adolescents' initiation of sexual intercourse.

• **Know where your teen is at all times, what he or she is doing and how to reach them.** Children without adult supervision are at much greater risk of truancy, stress, poor grades, risky behavior and substance abuse. Parents also need to know what their teens are really doing. Newport Beach clinical psychologist and adolescent specialist Jerry Weichman, Ph.D., explains, "I have seen so many highly invested and highly educated parents have no clue what is occurring with their teen behind the scenes as the teens have become very good at hiding it. It is imperative for parents to have monitoring software on their teen's phone and computer. This is the only true looking glass you are going to have into their world. It will enable you to catch situational issues before they become life problems and at the very least, validate to you as a parent that your child is okay which will enable you to feel more comfortable allowing them to have additional freedom and independence as they earn it."

• **Know your teen's friends and their parents.** Parental monitoring of peers plays a large role in reducing adolescent delinquent activity, including drug use and unsafe sexual activity. It is important to share similar values with the parents of your teen's friends regarding parental supervision, drugs, alcohol, driving, etc.

• **Maintain open communication with your child.** According to Joseph A. Califano, founder of the National Center on Addiction and Substance Abuse, parents must keep the lines of communication open in order to be effective drug prevention agents. This involves listening, addressing concerns calmly and affirming positive behavior and attitudes.

• **Set clear rules and consequences for violating those rules.** Explain the reasons to avoid drugs, alcohol, tobacco, risky sexual behavior and delinquent activity. Caring parents who provide rules and supervision can help to reduce adolescent delinquency. You are still the most important teacher your child will ever have. Use their mistakes or poor judgment as learning opportunities, not as indictments of their worth. Most of us learn important life lessons from our mistakes and poor choices- teens are the same. Legendary coach and mentor John Wooden tells parents to teach their children, "Be true to yourself. You know what is right. Don't let someone else decide for you." (Wooden and Jamison, 1997, p. 37).

• **Incorporate religious and spiritual practices into family life.** Youth who are religious are less likely to participate in delinquent activity.

• **Help your teen to understand their unique personalities, strengths and weaknesses.** Support your child's positive social interests and hobbies. Help them to identify their talents and unique temperament.

• **Find support as a parent of a teen.** This can be informal like friends, school, faith based or professional support. Others can help you maintain sense of perspective.

(For more ways to reduce the likelihood of risky teen behavior go to www.search-institute.org to see all 40 developmental assets.)

Sometimes, problems with your teen still arise, and if that occurs, you need to know what to do. Orange County juvenile and family law attorney Maureen Meehan Aplin states, "There are many warning signs for risky behavior and many underlying reasons that fuel the outcome of the behaviors. It is important for parents of teenagers to observe their children daily, question changes in behaviors, listen patiently to the rationale a teen gives for the changes, and to be present, forward thinking, and solution oriented when a teenager makes a mistake." If you have serious concerns about your teen, professional help may be needed.

Most teens successfully navigate adolescence and become productive young adults. Parents need to remember that. According to adolescent psychologist and author Michael Bradley, "It can get really messy, it can be quite painful, and it can be very scary. But these things all end, and like with raising teens, mostly everyone survives just fine."

When should you be Concerned?

How do you know what is normal for a teen going through so many changes and what is not? If their behavior is self-destructive or adversely affects others, then it is a problem. Below are some warning signs that you can be watchful for during the teen years.

Warning Signs

<u>Problem Behaviors</u> (Stay aware of these behaviors, if not changed these could lead to more serious problems)
- Entitlement
- Rationalized /minimizes bad behavior
- Lying
- Argumentative, defensive
- Non-compliance to rules
- Victim outlook
- Externalizing blame

<u>Serious</u> (Intervention may be needed to avoid a crisis)
- Social withdrawal
- Unsafe sexual behavior
- Abandonment of personal interests
- Frequent depression and discouragement
- Sudden changes in appearance
- Involved in gang activity (See Resources for more information.)
- Aggressive/violent/assaultive behavior
- Repeated threats, verbal or physical
- Impulse control problem
- Things missing around the house, unaccounted increase in money or possessions

<u>Critical</u> (Immediate intervention is required)
- Attempted suicide or threats of suicide
- Self-mutilation
- Trouble with the law
- Running away from home or threatening to run away
- Involvement in Cult activities
- Drug and Alcohol Use
- Serious problems at school (expulsion, truancies, multiple suspensions, falling way behind academically)
- Eating disorders; obsessed with their body image

Is (or has) your child demonstrating any of these behaviors? If so, which ones?

_____

_____

How are you addressing those areas of concern?

_____

_____

Tool # 3

Parenting Styles and Loving Your Children

Parenting Styles

It is important to remember that we are to be parents to our children. Children need us to be parents, not to be their friends. Your child needs his own friends and you need your own. The paradox of parenting is that if we do our job well, we eventually lose our job! It is *then* that we can be a friend to our children.

How we parent our children, i.e. our parenting style, has such a critical impact on the type of people our children will become, the type of lives they will lead and how they will raise their own children. This section will explain the different parenting styles and their impact on children.

Our parenting styles are largely a reflection of our own parents' parenting style and our natural instincts as parents. Your particular style is largely learned from the parent figures that raised you as a child, but like any learned behavior they can be unlearned, if you find you want to make changes in your parenting style. With conscious effort that is coupled with an effective replacement style that is practiced, adjustments to your parenting style can be made.

Parenting style captures two important elements of parenting: *parental responsiveness and parental demandingness* (Maccoby & Martin, 1983). Parental responsiveness (also referred to as parental warmth or supportiveness) refers to "the extent to which parents intentionally foster individuality, self-regulation, and self-assertion by being attuned, supportive, and acquiescent to children's special needs and demands" (Baumrind, 1991, p. 62). Parental demandingness (also referred to as behavioral control) refers to "the claims parents make on children to become integrated into the family whole, by their maturity demands, supervision, disciplinary efforts and willingness to confront the child who disobeys" (Baumrind, 1991, pp. 61-62).

What do you think is your own level of responsiveness and demandingness?

_____

_____

_____

From these 2 elements (parental responsiveness and parental

> *"Children desperately need to know –and to hear in ways they understand and remember –that they're loved and valued by mom and dad."*
> Paul Smalley

41

demandingness) arise 4 four primary parenting styles, although individuals often display a combination of styles, with one style predominating. These four styles are: *Indulgent* (permissive), *Authoritarian* (inflexible), *Authoritative* (flexible), and *Uninvolved* (disengaged). With each style comes your child's response which may lead to certain behavioral characteristics.

Parenting Styles and their Impacts on Children

Indulgent (Permissive): This style is demonstrated by the parent who allows children too much control and decision- making power. Parents with this style are afraid to set limits or guide their children adequately. Children tend to be impulsive, aggressive, lack independence and the ability to take responsibility for their actions.

Authoritative (Flexible): This parenting style is warm, affectionate, reasonable, and capable of good listening and is neither neglectful nor too permissive. This parent is comfortable with setting and enforcing limits, while including the child in the process.
The children whose parents have a flexible style of parenting have high self-esteem, are good problem solvers, and are achievement oriented. They are often excellent students, cooperative, and are basically content.

Authoritarian (Inflexible): The opposite of flexible parenting is demonstrated by controlling, rigid, and strict parenting. This style does not allow children to make mistakes, expects perfectionism and has unreasonable expectations. An inflexible style is unable to adjust their parenting style to a child's changing developmental stages.
Although the children are often well behaved, they tend to be followers and may suffer from low self-esteem, mood imbalances and anxiety.

Uninvolved (Disengaged): An uninvolved parent is emotionally detached or emotionally unavailable to their children. These parents do not set a lot of limits and may be less available to their children. Children tend to be needier, more aggressive, rebellious and suffer from low self-esteem. They may also be overachievers, people pleasers, perfectionists, and constantly seeking validation.

(Komen and Myers, 2000, pp. 260-261; Wicks-Nelson and Israel, 1991, p.28)

What style or combination of parenting styles did your parents display?

_____

_____

_____

What do you think is your parenting style?

_____
_____
_____

What style does your child's other parent/parental figure have?

_____
_____
_____

From your predominant parenting style, what characteristics have you observed in your child?

_____
_____
_____

Dynamics in relationships may lead your child to respond in a certain manner to a particular parenting style. Understanding your parenting style is important as it may help you to understand your child's responses to you and lead you to adjust your parenting style to better meet your child's needs.

Parental Warmth

Parental warmth (being responsive and supportive) has positive impacts on wellbeing even beyond childhood. Stossel (2013) summarizes the findings from the Grant Study, one of the longest running longitudinal studies of human development which began in 1938, which has followed 238 Harvard undergraduate men for 75 years.

The bottom line in this study was that what matters most in life are relationships. And the first and most significant relationship a child has is with his parents or parent figures.

The findings reveal the crucial role that parental warmth in childhood plays in happiness and other wellness indicators throughout life. This study found that the warmth of a child's relationship with his (her) mother matters long into adulthood, and in addition, was found to be correlated with higher incomes and effectiveness at work. Children who had poor childhood relationships with their mothers were more likely to develop dementia as they aged.

Warm childhood relationship with fathers correlated with lower levels of adult anxiety, greater enjoyment of vacations, and increased life satisfaction at age 75.

Warm, supportive, and responsive relationships with your children involve opening yourself up emotionally to your children, being empathic toward them, and demonstrating your love for them with your words and actions. Ralph Waldo Emerson eloquently summed it up with this thought, "Material things are not gifts but apologies for gifts. The only true gift is a portion of thyself."

How do you give of yourself to your children?

_____

_____

_____

"Love and acceptance are essential for healthy child development, to building feelings of self-worth and self-esteem. Affection is the most crucial of all the influences provided in the home. If we get this part right, we're already 80 percent successful as parents" (Kennedy, 2001, p.151). Children need love, acceptance, and affection *communicated* and *demonstrated* to them consistently. (See Resources for more information.)

How do you show your love, acceptance and affection to your child?

_____

_____

_____

No matter what your child's age or developmental stage, being a warm parent to your children *will always mean listening to them*. Listening is love in action. Are you a good listener to your child? Share a recent time when you made a conscious effort to really listen to your child.

_____

_____

_____

Loving your children

We understand how parenting styles affect our children, and how they need a balance of responsiveness and demandingness from us. Another way to say this is that children need love and limits.

But other than meeting our children's basic needs and protecting them from harm, love and limits are what we need to provide for them so that can they grow up healthy, well-adjusted and live meaningful lives. (Limits are covered in our chapter on discipline.) Loving your children is so necessary for their health and wellbeing and is such a life changing experience for us as parents, that a clear understanding of what loving your children entails is critical in being able to provide that for them.

As parents, our first and foremost responsibility is to love them. We find that most parents eagerly say they love their children and we are convinced that they do, but we are not the ones that need to be convinced! Your children need to feel your love in a way that is meaningful to them; if they don't feel it from you, they will be left without the necessary foundation for their sense of self-worth and emotional connectedness.

Your love for your children must be understood and felt by them. As parents and caregivers we have the privilege and responsibility to provide this for them. In addition to setting limits for them (See Ch. 7), this is largely done by consistently demonstrating love, staying attentive and being emotionally attuned to them.

Demonstrating Love

There are so many ways to demonstrate love and affection to your children but what is most important is that you *love your child without conditions placed upon them or their performance.*

One of the ways children know you love them is by the time you spend with them.

Beyond the time you spend, it is important to demonstrate your love and open yourself up emotionally to your children. Common examples of this include sharing of yourself with your children, showing physical affection, listening to them, caring for their needs, holding them accountable for their actions, and everyday interactions where you are present and attuned to them. Talking, singing, playing, eating, cooking, reading, shopping, enjoying nature, or simply sitting close to each other and working on tasks together can help to create the bond that leads to healthy emotional connectedness between you and your child.

When you were a child how did your parents or caregivers demonstrate love to you?

_____

_____

_____

List 3 ways that you *demonstrate* your love for your child.

_____

_____

_____

How do you show physical affection (loving touch) to your child?

_____

_____

_____

Do a loving act for them everyday, even and especially when they don't deserve it! It shows them that you love them no matter what. This is not to be confused with being permissive, indulgent, or not following through on discipline.

We all know we need to be involved in our children's lives. But what does that actually mean for *us*? It is important to appreciate the unique needs of your child (or children) balanced against the realities of your life, including your energy level, family dynamics and personal needs.

In making choices for our lives concerning the time we spend with our children, it is important to remember that we are making invaluable deposits in their memory banks. What memories are you giving to your children?

_____

_____

_____

Being present with your children is a conscious choice of self-sacrifice. You acknowledge and are willing to put the investment of your time, energy and heart into your child *even when you don't feel like it and even when you are not getting anything in return.* It is a decision to value the human being that has been entrusted to you.

Savor the moments with your child. Find something to love about them everyday. Some days this will be easier than other days. What do you love about your children today?

_____

_____

_____

What you *think* about your child has a tremendous impact on your actions and attitudes toward him. Finding and recalling something positive may help you cherish your child and help you "hang in there" when you, as a parent, are struggling with a challenging child or a difficult situation and would rather run away from it all!

What positive memory comes to mind when you think of either your children or how parenting has made your life more meaningful?

_____

_____

_____

Staying Attentive

Let your child be your teacher. This statement is not as absurd as it may sound. Your child is constantly giving you feedback on his health, feelings, thoughts, needs, desires, and limits. Being aware of what your child is telling you about *who he is* and how he is experiencing life can help you respond in a loving, sensitive and effective manner.

Sometimes we need to look at our children with new eyes. "Children need to be seen and known by their parents. It isn't enough to know our children's preferences and a few qualities about them. They need to be witnessed for who they are, deep down. Otherwise, their sense of self can be diminished, even eradicated-and this creates a deep sense of loss and a feeling of disconnectedness from one's true identity" (Wilson, 1999, p. 42).

Your love and your time are the two of the most important things that you can give your children. It may sound obvious, but we can't give our children the love, acceptance and affection they need if we are not *present*. One of the most important aspects of parenting is simply "showing up!" "*Being there*" is the first step in letting your child know that you love them and that they have value. It is important to remember that no matter what your child's age or developmental stage they need to *feel* loved and valued in order to grow to become healthy, confident, independent and caring adults.

How we spend our time and resources reflects our priorities. Children know if they are important by the time we spend with them.

Is spending time with your child (or children) a priority? Explain what you do that demonstrates they are a priority in your life. How are you letting your child know that you love him by the time you spend with him/her?

_____

_____

_____

Spending time with your children does not necessarily mean extravagant trips to amusement parks or fancy dinners at expensive restaurants. It is more about being present and available to them. Of course, with a younger child, closer physical contact is needed more than with an older child.

It is vital that you remember that, although, your child may appear more independent as they get older or as an adolescent even express a resistance towards your involvement in their life, *your involvement in their lives is critical to their healthy development*. Your level of involvement, however, should adapt to their needs, growing maturity and autonomy.

Knowing you are there (and being there) if they should need you helps children trust themselves and to become more independent. They need to *know* that they can depend on you. Depending on the age of your child/children, how do you let them know that you "are there" for them?

_____

_____

_____

Being Emotionally Attuned

Being emotionally attuned to your child means being aware and responding appropriately to his emotional states, in a supportive and nurturing manner. This is crucial to not only the bond between a parent and child, but also plays a critical role in healthy child development, including the development of the circuitry involved in emotional regulation.

As children are "hard wired" to emotionally connect with their parents or caregiver, if parents are too stressed out and not attuned to their children emotionally and responding appropriately, this lack of connection creates stress for the child. If this stress is long-lasting and especially during critical early years of development, it can impact the developing brain, which can lead to problems with attention, emotional regulation, and other difficulties as they grow up. And it is the temperamentally sensitive child that will be more affected by a stressed-out atmosphere in the family. (Mate, 2011)

In order for the circuitry of emotional regulation to develop, there needs to be a certain kind of atmosphere—primarily a non-stressed parent that is able to be attuned to the child. A parent may not be attuned to their children for many reasons; this does not mean they don't love their children, but it does mean that they are not providing the calmed, attuned attention that a child needs.

Reasons for a parent being stressed out and therefore unable to pay attention and respond to the emotional needs of their child are quite numerous. It can come from unnecessary pressures we place on ourselves and our children, conditions in society and changing family structures, which can lead to feelings of isolation (Mate, 2011).

But it can also include factors such as a parent's mental illness, physical illness, family history of violence, immaturity, financial hardships, poor coping skills, unresolved trauma, personal crisis, physical absence, or addictions among others.

Is your level of stress interfering with your ability to be attuned to your child?

Are you aware of and responding to the emotional needs of your child? Give an example.

_____

_____

_____

Fostering Self Determination

Loving your child also means helping to prepare them adulthood and living independently. Self-determination is of extreme importance for all children, but especially for those with special needs. This is a quality that you will need to nurture in your child. Children who develop this quality have a sense of control over their lives and can set goals and work to attain them.

Youth with disabilities who also have high levels of self-determination are more likely to become adults who are:
- Employed
- Satisfied with their lives
- Living independently, or with outside support

Here are some tips to help your child become self-determined:

- As early as possible, give your child opportunities to make choices and encourage your child to express wants and wishes. For instance, these could be choices about what to wear, what to eat, and how much help with doing things your child wants from you.
- Strike a balance between being protective and supporting risk-taking. Learn to let go a little and push your child out into the world, even though it may be a little scary.
- Guide children toward solving their own problems and making their own choices. For instance, if your child has a problem at school, offer a listening ear and together brainstorm possible solutions. To the extent that your child can, let your child decide on the plan and the back-up plan. (Illnesses and Disabilities, 2009)

What have you done (or are doing) to help your child to become self-determined?

_____

_____

_____

Being loving, attentive and emotionally attuned to your child are necessary to healthy child development, as is helping them to be self-determined. Yet, that is only part of what children need to mature. Research identifies additional "assets" that are correlated with healthy child development. The Search Institute has identified 40 Developmental Assets® (external and internal assets) that are the building blocks of healthy child development. (See Resources)

Tool # 4
Role Modeling for Our Children

> *"Children have never been very good at listening to their elders, but they have never failed to imitate them."*
> James Baldwin

Understanding the Parent Role Model

Being a good role model for your children does not mean you have to be perfect. It does mean, however, *being the kind of person you want your child to be*. It means leading by example. It means teaching your children how to handle difficult situations, how to be honest, how to be kind, how to be brave, how to say sorry, how to communicate effectively and how to love (Parenting Guidelines, 2011, Role of Parents). Being a positive role model means that we as parents need to look at our own behavior, how we handle situations, and the messages we are sending to our children through our words, as well as our nonverbal communication, including body language and tone of voice. Remember, children tend to become what they witness and hear.

2 simple tips to be a good parental role model

- Model the good behavior and character you expect your children to adopt
- Abide by the rules you set.

Give an example when you modeled good the behavior and character that you want your children to have.

_____

_____

_____

The Past is not the Present

Children help us grow up. Some of us do this more willingly than others. Some of us may find certain areas where we embrace adulthood and other areas where we are reluctant to part with an immature behavior or outlook.

For some of us being a good role model may seem more difficult due to our level of maturity, past choices and lifestyles. All of us have come to this point in our lives with some regrets and disappointments with some of the choices and decisions we have made. Some of us may have more than others. It is helpful to remember that our past is just that- the past. Even if you indulged in excesses and inappropriate behavior and relationships in the past, you are a parent today and your child needs you to be a positive role model. Your past does not have to determine how you act today- you do! It is important that you not allow past mistakes or painful childhood experiences to dictate *who you are today and how you parent.*

There are things that you could do when you were childless that may not be appropriate when you had children. What changes have you made in your lifestyle since you have had children?

_____

_____

_____

Because your children are looking to you as their role model, are there any aspects of your current lifestyle that may need changing or warrants careful attention? What might those be?

_____

_____

_____

As a child, what positive role modeling did your parents do? What negative role modeling did you observe?

_____

_____

_____

If you find it is difficult to make changes or move forward because of your past experiences and choices, you may need additional professional help. Remember that smart people get help when they need it! If you think you may benefit from additional help, please find it. You and your children will greatly benefit from the insights and healing that may be found in accessing outside resources or in a therapeutic relationship.

Even parents who have made many mistakes or who have not prioritized their families as they should, should never stop trying. Children are resilient. It is never too late to be a better parent while your child is alive. In what ways do you think you need to be a better parent? In what ways have you improved your parenting?

_____

_____

_____

Learning to forgive yourself is vital to being the parent your child needs today. Mistakes are great teachers for not only your children, but for yourself, too. In what aspect of your parenting do you need to forgive yourself? In what aspects of your parenting do you need to ask forgiveness from your child?

_____

_____

_____

Gender Roles

It is understood that girls learn from their mothers and other female role models in their lives how to be a young woman. If you have a daughter, who are her primary female role models? (Include yourself if you are her mother/guardian.)

_____

_____

_____

From these role models, what is she learning about being a woman?

_____

_____

_____

The same goes for boys- they learn how to be a man from their fathers and other male role models. If you have a son, who are his primary male role models? (Include yourself if you are his father/guardian.)

_____

_____

_____

From these role models, what is he learning about being a man?

_____

_____

_____

Unfortunately, many children do not have fathers as active parts of their lives and this creates problems for both the female and male child. Father figures are as crucial to healthy child development as mothers are.

The Importance of a Positive Male Role Model

Many boys today do not know what it means to be a man because they don't have a man in their lives. Many children will go to bed tonight without saying goodnight to their father because he just isn't there.

Nearly one-fourth of America's children live in mother-only families. Of the children living with their mothers, 35 percent never see their father and 24 percent see their fathers less than once a month.

These children live with a woman and more than likely, they are taught by a woman at school. Where do they see and interact with positive male role models? Or, if they are a boy how do they learn what it means to be a man? Television? Movies? On the street?

Even in homes where the father is present research shows that the average father spends less than 10 minutes a day one-on-one with his child. We are living in a society where emotional and spiritual father-lessness is becoming the norm. Many of today's fathers did not have positive role models to show them what it means to be a father to a child, so they are not there to show their children what it means to be a father.

No matter how great a mother is, she cannot replace what a father provides to a child. Irrefutable research shows that mothers typically are nurturing, soft, gentle, comforting, protective and emotional. Fathers tend to be challenging, prodding, loud, playful, encourage risk taking, and physical. Children need a *balance of protection and reasonable risk taking*. If a positive male role model is not present in the life of a child there is a void in this area. Children who live in this environment are more likely to be involved in criminal activity, premarital sexual activity, do poorer in school and participate in unhealthy activities.

Studies have shown that involvement of a father or a positive male role model in the lives of children has profound effects on them. Father-child interaction promotes a child's physical well-being, perceptual ability and competency for relating with others. These children also demonstrate greater ability to take initiative and evidence self-control.

(The Importance of a Positive Role Model, n.d. p. 1)

If you are a single mother or father, what can you do to make a positive difference for your child?

> • If you are a mother you can encourage the involvement of positive male role models in the life of your child.
> • If you are a non-custodial dad you can make the effort to visit with your child more often and be intentional about teaching them important life lessons.

What are you modeling today?

Being a parent means that we are constant role models whether we like it or not! Your children are observing and learning from your life about how to be an adult, parent, spouse, partner, employee, friend, neighbor, relative, etc. One of the most important things they are learning from you is how to treat people, and the relationships that are the most significant to you, will have the greatest impact on learning this.

If (and when) you are in a committed relationship, how you treat your partner and how he treats you provides your child with a template for his relationships.

What is your child learning in regards to how partners treat one another?

_____

_____

_____

Your children are also learning from you how to deal (or not deal) with life's challenges and disappointments. In addition, you are teaching them what is of value, by how you spend your time, energy, and resources.

Kids learn by imitating. They will follow your lead in how they deal with anger, solve problems and work through difficult feelings.

So how should parents teach their children to handle difficult feelings? First, it is necessary that you must first learn to understand and appropriately manage your own feelings such as anger, fear and sadness. Second, nothing can be taught without the proper application. Demonstrating honest and healthy management of feelings will provide the best role model for your children. Anything you verbally "teach" in addition to what you live will either confirm it or, if inconsistent with your actions, will confuse them. Remember- what you are *doing*, not saying, is the most powerful teacher.

What are you modeling to your children about dealing with disappointment?

_____

_____

_____

When you are angry, what do your children learn about how to deal with it?

_____

_____

_____

How you handle conflict is especially important because, for some of you, you are in a conflict ridden relationship at this time. What are your children learning, from your words and actions, about dealing with conflict?

Children will greatly benefit from having a parent who has learned the art of having respectful arguments. When you and your spouse, partner or co-parent disagree, it is important to have appropriate boundaries and not to "carry on" in front of the children. Children have great ears for things that you don't want them to hear! Present a united front with the children so they don't see a window to manipulate one parent over the other.

Share a time when you had a respectful argument with your spouse, partner or your child's other parent or caregiver.

_____

_____

_____

Children see and hear pretty much everything, even when we don't think they do. Sometimes it takes our child imitating our inappropriate behavior for us to realize that they are watching and learning all the time. Find a humorous example of when your child imitated your conduct or attitude.

_____

_____

_____

Describe a time when your child imitated your behavior that you found troubling.

_____

_____

_____

Some parents make the mistake of thinking they have to act like a cool friend to their children. Being a positive role model does not mean being a "cool" parent. What your children need from you is for you to be a parent, not a buddy! What your child needs is for you to stay true to your values and ethics in a society where morals are often in a free fall. Your role is to "stand as lighthouse, as constant points of references" (Bradley, 2002, p.125), especially as he navigates the often turbulent waters of adolescence.

What are some of your beliefs and values? How are those demonstrated in your life? Give an example.

_____

_____

_____

It is important to take the time to seriously answer these questions, as they will guide your life and your parenting. Having clarity on your beliefs and values will help you to act in a way that is consistent with those ideals, even when it is difficult. And that is actually when your beliefs, values and personal character are truly demonstrated.

Share a time when you held fast to your beliefs or values in a difficult time?

_____

_____

_____

Being a Role Model in all Areas of your Child's Development

There are so many areas in a child's life that you shape and influence that it can feel a bit overwhelming at times. Sometimes it is hard to know all that you should to help them become healthy, well-adjusted children and young adults. A useful guide is Bright Futures: Guidelines for Health Supervision of Infants, Children, and Adolescent, published by the National Center for Education in Maternal and Child Health. This "Anticipatory Guidance "is a good "checklist" to help you remember what important things you should be teaching your children and at what age. Topics vary for each stage, but include areas such as nutrition, fitness, safety, school success, responsibility, family, independence, community and as they enter puberty and adolescence topics such as prevention of substance use and abuse and sexuality. (See Resources.)

Having a healthy, meaningful life entails sacrifice and hard work. We need to teach this to our children and the best way to teach this to our children is to model it! Live the behaviors and traits you want your children to adopt. Every minute of your existence you are modeling to your children. That sounds pretty overwhelming, but the important thing to remember is, what are you modeling *most* of the time? That will stick.

Tool # 5
Empathy

> *"Empathy is caring for the sould of another."*
> Paul Wong, Ph.D.

Emotions and Our Life

Empathy is one of the most important skills to have in being a good parent as well as co-parenting with an ex-partner. Empathy is the ability to feel the feelings of another so that we can relate to them on an emotional level. When we are better able to do this, we better understand the needs of our children and those that also share the responsibility of parenting with us.

The expression of emotion is often passed down from our parents, guardians, or caregivers as children. Many of us often express, or lack the ability to express, our emotions based on how we learned to do so in childhood. Some of us are very good at knowing how we feel and expressing it, while others struggle to do so. It is crucial to express emotion in order to relate to those around us. Our ability to know how we are feeling as well as our ability to accurately sense the feelings of those around us help us to make positive connections with others. This characteristic is often called "empathy."

Emotions are what allow us to grow in love. They are also the stuff of poetry, art, and music. Emotions fill us with a sense of connection to others. In many ways, emotions make life worth living. How we experience the world, relate to others, and find meaning in life are dependent upon how we regulate our emotions.

People who have the ability to understand and regulate their emotions as well as sense and understand the emotions of others are said to have a quality called "emotional intelligence" (EQ), a new term coined by psychologists. Research shows that persons with high "EQ" excel in leadership, sales, academic performance, marriage, friendships, and overall health. Two of the most important traits associated with emotional intelligence are empathy and social awareness.

Why Empathy is Important

Nature developed our emotions over millions of years of evolution and they serve an important social function. This function is that of allowing one person to have a sense of the mental state of another person. *Empathy is the capacity to feel another person's experience. As one English author wrote: "To empathize is to see with the eyes of another, to hear with the ears of another, to feel with the heart of another."*

Empathy requires knowing the perspective of others and being able to see things from the value and belief system of the other person. Being empathic is the ability to fully immerse oneself in another's viewpoint, yet be able to remain wholly apart.

Empathy is important in the world because lack of it leads to poor communication and a failing to understand others. Empathy on a personal level is important because it allows us to understand social interactions and to anticipate the behavior of others. Empathy also allows others to understand us; when we are with highly empathetic people, we feel felt by the other—that is, that they are emotionally attuned to us and can see the world from our point of view.

Children need our empathy. This is a skill that children must feel from you. To them life is very big and often overwhelming. A lack of empathy towards our children leads to low self-esteem, feelings of isolation and of being misunderstood.

The California Department of Education cites the benefits for children being treated with empathy. Research has shown a correlation between empathy and prosocial behavior (Eisenberg, 2000). In particular, prosocial behaviors, such as helping, sharing, and comforting or showing concern for others, illustrate the development of empathy (Zahn-Waxler and others, 1992) and how the experience of empathy is thought to be related to the development of moral behavior (Eisenberg, 2000).

Lack of Empathy

Lack of empathy leads to all sorts of problems in our world. Nations go to war, people get killed, and couples divorce- all for a lack of empathy and understanding. Our prisons are filled with people who don't have the capacity to feel their victim's pain or suffering. This lack of empathy keeps them from feeling what it is like to be hurt.

A lack of empathy is a sign that people think only of themselves. These people are concerned only with their own ideas and feelings — not others. They push only their own issues while not seeing the needs of others. While children are naturally self-interested, it is our job as parents to not only have empathy for them, but also to teach them to have empathy for others, including modeling empathy for their other parent.

Have you been able to have empathy for your child's other parent? Not having it will not help you or your children. Share a time when you had empathy for your child's other parent.

_____

_____

_____

Why Social Awareness is Important

Some people seem to go through life almost oblivious to the impact they are having on others in their world. Often they upset people at work or in their family due to their behavior but seem stunned when they find out that people are reacting to them in a negative way. Lacking empathy, they aren't able to "read" others enough to see what impact their behavior is having, so they keep on doing the same thing —which unfortunately keeps getting them the same result.

One way to increase awareness is to operate on two levels in your mind at the same time; in computer language, it is like running the main program but also having another program running silently in the background. The main program is what you are trying to communicate (for instance, "you need to complete your homework before you go outside and play"). The other program is imagining how you look or sound to your child while you are delivering the main message.

The following technique may be helpful; when talking to your child, imagine there is video camera (or someone you respect) in the corner of the room recording your behavior. Ask yourself:

• How am I looking right now from my child's perspective?
• How am I being seen from the viewpoint of my child?
• Is the message I'm delivering the same one they are receiving?

How Can You Learn to Be More Empathetic?

The feeling of empathy starts at a very young age and is probably developed by the manner in which infant and parent are attached to each other emotionally. This attachment is formed by parents or caretakers responding to the infant's feelings in a positive way so that the infant learns to trust and to be concerned with the feelings of other people. Babies with secure attachment to their parents have a head start on less fortunate babies who have parents that produce insecurity or uncertainty in their children.

From birth, a baby can become upset when it hears another baby crying; this may be the groundwork for later empathy. Studies show that babies as young as nine months old can be aware of other babies' pain and suffering—definitely a sign of empathy.

Empathy is built through increased awareness of yourself. "To be sensitive is to feel the thoughts and hearts of others as only you would want yours felt." (Anonymous) The more you understand yourself and your emotions, the better you will be in understanding, appreciating, and relating to the feelings of others. As you develop empathic ability, you will find it more and more difficult to stay angry at people.

By showing empathy to your children, you are helping them to feel understood, to understand their own emotions and to begin to relate to the feelings of others. It is important to foster sensitivity to your child's needs and feelings so he can be empathic towards himself and others.

It is natural to become so absorbed in the everyday stressors and responsibilities of adulthood and parenting that we can forget that children also have stressors, too. We sometimes forget this and may treat their problems and feelings as insignificant because as an adult those problems may appear unimportant to us. For example, most of us wouldn't throw a tantrum if we didn't have our security blanket at bedtime, but to a very young child a security blanket may help him feel safe and secure during certain periods of his life. The blanket means something very different and more significant to him than it does to you.

What is an example when you had empathy for a difficult feeling or a problem your child was experiencing?

_____

_____

_____

Value what matters to your child. Take the time to listen with your heart, not just your ears. You will become aware of and understand what matters to him. Do not ridicule something that is important or troubling him. Do not belittle or minimize his concerns and fears; instead learn to soothe and guide your child. (This is especially important for a sensitive child.) For example, if your child is petrified of dogs or spiders, do not criticize him for his fears, but be gentle in guiding him through his fears. How have you demonstrated this?

_____

_____

_____

Apologize when you blow it! Saying "I am sorry" to our children may be difficult for many of us, especially for those of us who had inflexible (authoritarian) parents as a child. Uttering those words may lead us to feel as if we are incompetent parents. Nothing could be further from the truth! Acknowledging our failings or mistakes does not mean we are incompetent. It simply means we are human!

You most likely want your child to learn to acknowledge their failings. They will best learn this from seeing you model it. Preaching isn't nearly as effective as living it.
Is there a recent example when you apologized to your child?

_____

_____

_____

Remember, you won't ever do everything right and you will never be a perfect parent, no matter how hard you try. Some parents may think they are handing the "reigns of authority" to a child when they apologize for their own poor behavior or unkind words, but apologizing can actually produce the opposite effect. It will generate respect from your children as they see you acknowledge that you make mistakes, too.

It is easy to act poorly around our children because we do not generally fear negative consequences from them and can easily justify how we treat them. It doesn't matter how you can justify your actions; if you feel you have done something that was not necessary and it hurt your child—*apologize*! Your children will learn that their feelings matter. It also demonstrates the proper amount of humility and an appropriate response when we have acted poorly. Apologizing when you have "blown it" creates an environment where your children will apologize more freely when they have hurt someone or made a bad decision. Remember, you are setting the standard for how they should treat others and how others should treat them.

Did you (or do you need to) apologize to your child for a recent action or unkind words? If so, what did/ would you say?

_____
_____
_____

Promoting Empathy in Your Children

As parents we can actively promote or inhibit the development of empathy in our children. Cotton (n.d.) explains what parents can do to either promote or inhibit the development of empathy in children.

Parenting practices that promote empathy in your children include:
- Explaining to children the effects of their behavior on others
- Pointing out to children that they have the power to make others happy by being kind and generous to them
- Modeling empathic, caring behavior
- Mothers demonstrating responsive, nonpunitive, nonauthoritarian behavior to their preschool children
- Encouraging school age children to discuss their feelings and problems with you
- Explaining to children who have hurt or distressed others why their behavior is harmful and giving them suggestions for making amends to those hurt

Which of the practices, above, do you demonstrate? Give an example.

_____
_____
_____

Parenting practices that inhibit the development of empathy in children:
- Threats and physical punishments aimed at inducing children to "behave properly"
- Inconsistent behavior towards children's expression of emotional needs or rejection/withdrawal in response to those needs
- Home situations in which children's parent is abused by the other parent, significant other or sibling.
- Bribes or extrinsic rewards given to children to elicit good behavior (p. 8).

Another way to think about how to be empathic toward your children is to think about how you would want to be treated if you were a child. If this is an area where your own parents lacked sensitivity, treat your child and discipline her the way you would have wanted to be treated or as someone you respect would do it. Make it a habit to observe effective, empathic parenting and ineffective, unempathic parenting as you go through your day- at the grocery store, at the park, or at your child's school. Incorporate appropriate parenting skills and empathic behavior into your parenting.

Do not forget that your child has never been the age she is. The younger, more immature or personally challenged she is, the more powerless she may feel and the greater her need for your empathy.

In order to have empathy for your child you need to have it for yourself as a parent! Having empathy for ourselves helps us to extend it to our children. Understanding that there are reasons for your own poor behavior can help you to not judge yourself, others or your children harshly.

State an example when you witnessed someone else's poor parenting.

_____
_____
_____

What could that parent have done differently?

_____
_____
_____

What do you think could lead a parent to behave in the manner you observed?

_____
_____
_____

Think about a time when you did not handle a situation well with your child. Were you out to cause harm to your child? Probably not. Usually when people are behaving poorly, it's because they don't have the strength or resources to deal with their problems.

Cite an example when you did not handle something well with your child. What was the underlying reason?

_____

_____

_____

Empathy builds and strengthens relationships. Simply put, empathy allows us to connect with another person. Empathic communication and listening is much more than simply verbalizing our thoughts and hearing another's words. In order to connect on a deep level with another person we must value the person we are trying to connect with, try to understand them and listen with empathy.

The following sections explore specifically how to be an empathic listener and how to communicate with empathy. Connecting with another person takes time, energy, risk, and an open heart, yet there is no closeness and intimacy without that. It is always in our closest relationships where we find the most meaning and fulfillment in our lives.

Who do you "connect" with? Who makes you feel valued and understood?

_____

_____

_____

Empathic Listening

Empathic listening is a type of listening that goes further than ordinary listening. This type of listening uses another person's point of view to see the world as others see it. It provides a higher level of understanding of how others feel.

Empathic listening is not a skill that most people have, but it can be developed with practice. Empathic listening is much more than just hearing. It is listening while you suspend your normal "filters" that determines what you hear. Everyone has these filters. If your "filter" is different from another's, you may "hear" the exact same message in a different way than he or she does.

What are some common filters that influence what we hear?

Filter 1 – "The Right/Wrong" Filter
Using this, you listen for evidence that what your child is saying is wrong and you are right. If you are indeed listening to justify your position, you can hardly be listening with empathy.

Filter 2 – "Loved/Not Loved" Filter
With this, we completely miss the point of what our child might be

trying to communicate, because all we are listening for is "do they still love me?" or "are they going to leave me?"

Filter 3 – "Criticism/Put-Down" Filter

Any complaint or problem your child has is heard as a personal put-down or criticism of us, rather than a legitimate complaint the child may have. For example, your child says (after you do not grant his request for a toy at the store), "You never buy me anything." What you hear is: "If I made more money and I was more adequate as a parent my child wouldn't be upset with me."

Filter 4 – "What Am I Going to Say Next?" Filter

This is listening, but with your answer running. Your real goal with this type of listening is to "one-up" your child, to prepare a comeback, to have a better story, to promote your self-interest, or to prove him wrong.

Filter 5 – "Get to the Point" Filter

Maybe you've noticed that some people's conversations are like a bullet train-—direct and to the destination—while others' are like a long trip down the Amazon River, taking in all the tributaries and scenery. If you only listen for "get to the point," you might miss important information that helps you understand how your child experiences his or her world. People who use this filter are often very impatient.

Empathic listening leads to a better understanding of our children's feelings and leads to fewer misunderstandings in almost all situations. Good listening is a valuable tool in building trust with our children and winning their respect, especially as they mature and become more independent.

Empathic Communication

Empathic communication requires awareness of both the messages you are sending and the messages you are receiving from your child. Some of the message is delivered or received with words while the majority of the message (probably 80%) through nonverbal communication. Let's start with the words and phrases we use to communicate. Avoid barriers to effective communication because they make it difficult for you to listen to your children with empathy.

Barriers to Effective Communication

(1) **Commanding** uses phrases like "You must…" or "You have to…" Exercising your parental authority does not need to include acting like a drill sergeant! Of course, with children you will need to be authoritative, but that does not mean taking on an authoritarian style of parenting. Constantly using "commanding" approaches to communicate to your child shows harshness and a lack of appreciation for the child's feelings and emotions. When you need to demand something from your child, and your requests are not followed, use commanding type of language sparingly- it will have more of an impact than if you use it often.

(2) **Browbeating** uses phrases like "If you don't, then…" or "You bet-

ter or else…" This is tantamount to threatening a child. Do not threaten what you do not intend to carry out. If you are stating a consequence that will occur if an action occurs (or does not occur), make sure you have thought it through and then follow through calmly.

(3) **"Shoulding" your children** uses phrases like "It is your duty to…," "You should…," or "You ought to…" It is better to explain what you want/need your child to do (or not do), than use language to induce guilt and shame. Again- these are phrases that should be used sparingly.

(4) **Scolding** uses phrases like "Let me tell you why you are wrong…," or "Do you realize…" It is important when correcting or disciplining your child, to be specific, express your concerns or disappointments, but avoid overly moralizing or being too judgmental.

(5) **Giving constant unrequested advice** uses phrases like "What I would do is…" or "It would be best if you…"As you guide your child throughout his life, you will, of course, give advice, but badgering constantly is what you want to avoid.

(6) **Moral judging** uses phrases like "You are bad/lazy". This makes a child feel like their worth is conditional and their character is being judged.

(7) **Playing psychiatrist** uses phrases like "You're just trying to get attention…" or "I know what you need…" This barrier assumes you know exactly what the child is experiencing, thinking, and feeling. (You don't.) It also inhibits your child from sharing the thoughts and feelings that are necessary to stay connected with him.

Which of these may be causing barriers to communicating with your child?

_____

_____

_____

In addition to avoiding these known barriers to empathic communication, you should also be aware of your nonverbal messages such as:

• **Facial expressions:** The language of our emotions is spoken by our face—not with the words that come out of our mouths but with expressions formed by our facial muscles. Researchers have found that 43 muscles create 10,000 visible facial configurations of which 3,000 are meaningful in terms of expressing emotion.

These emotional expressions are universal and do not depend on any particular learning or culture that we are in. This means that people around the world have the same expressions on their faces, revealing their emotions. These emotions can be read accurately by people in different parts of the world from very diverse cultures. This fact can help unite people because emotional expression serves as a common thread among all human beings.

• **Touch** is a very basic way to connect with other human beings which, like facial expression is a natural form of communication that everyone understands. The sense of connection that children feel to their parents has a lot to do with the sense of touch, even as they get older. Touch can be a powerful, trusted way to communicate both your feelings and also show that you understand how your child is feeling. It is important that you touch and show affection to your child regularly. The right touch at the right time can say a lot—even though it may last only a moment.

• **Eye gaze/contact** is an important communication tool in learning to feel empathy for another human being. It has been said that the eyes are the windows to the soul. Eye contact helps you feel "connected" to another and also helps the others feel connected to you. Eye contact is also very useful when we want to make sure we are being heard. Eye contact means different things in different cultures, however, it is not quite the "universal" language that touch and facial expressions are.

• **Voice Tone** refers to the manner in which a verbal statement is presented, i.e., its rhythm, breathiness, hoarseness, or loudness. Your tone of voice reflects emotion and mood. It may also carry social information, as in a sarcastic, superior, or submissive manner of speaking. Many voice qualities are universal across all human cultures (though they are also subject to cultural modification and shaping). For instance, adults use higher pitched voices to speak to infants and young children. The softer pitch is innately "friendly" and suggests a non aggressive, non hostile pose. To increase empathy, it is extremely important to be mindful of the message being conveyed by your voice tone. When relating to your children, be aware of your tone and ask yourself if it is consistent with the words you are using. If your words and tone are not in agreement, your child will be responding to your tone as much as or more than to your words.

• **Stance and physical appearance** communicate to us much about how a person is feeling and also gives others non-verbal messages regarding our emotional states. How close someone stands to us, for instance, may be a message as to their positive feelings for us. Folded arms may signal defensiveness; clenched hands on hips with outstretched elbows and a legs-apart stance is typical of a parent scolding their children and may remind us of being scolded. Be very mindful when disciplining your child that your physical stature, especially for men, if coupled with an angry countenance can be overpowering and feel overwhelming to a child.

Acceptance

Acceptance is the ability to see that others have a right to their feelings and viewpoints. We must allow our children to have feelings without telling them how they should feel or think. Acceptance of our children's feelings is not easy unless we understand that all people, even children, have their own feelings. Empathetic parents understand that feelings may be difficult to control and that children need to be taught how to express their feelings in an appropriate manner.

How have you taught your child to express his feelings in an appropriate manner?

_____

_____

_____

It is also important to keep in mind that children, because of their immaturity, have unique limitations and vulnerabilities. Understanding this and being more tolerant of your child is a major step toward empathy.

Tool # 6
Communication

This tool is just a good, basic lesson in effective communication skills. It will help you in many areas of your life, not just as a parent or co-parent, but also in business and other relationships.

Effective communication is one of the most important skills needed to be a good parent as well as interact well with your child's other parent, and/or blended family situation.

Infant, toddlers, young children, and teenagers are like sponges growing up. Everything they say verbally and nonverbally is learned. Of course, genetics plays a part, but by and large, we are a product of our environment.

Children learn how to communicate from their family of origin. And, as parents, you may need to improve your communication skills so that you can either be a better parent, maintain the rights to parent your child, or better get along with your child's other parent. Good communication skills are important not just for your benefit, but also to teach your children.

Good communication skills are the foundation to having a great relationship with your children. Effective parents communicate well and are approachable. Communication is the tool that links us with our children and allows them to be connected to us.

Communication is such a part of our ability to function as humans that we may assume that we are effective communicators just because we are talking! Effective communication with our children involves more than simply talking *to* them. Communication involves proper timing and *both* talking and listening. Children need to be spoken to, of course, the ability to use words allows us to express ourselves and our feelings. But it also involves listening with our hearts and being aware of the actual message that we and our children (or the others) are actually communicating.

Assertive Communication

The way we communicate or the style we use to communicate is often learned from much earlier experiences in our lives when our language skills were newly formed. Think about your family's style of communication for a moment. Is your style similar to any of theirs? Most of us tend to communicate in a way that was adaptive in the environment

> *"Communication is not just about the words you used, but also about the manner of speaking, body language, and above all, the effectiveness with which you listen."*
> www.everychild-matters.gov

we grew up, but it may have become problematic in our lives today. For many of us, our style of communication can leave us with unmet needs, unexpressed emotion, and damaging effects on those around us. It is important to understand that there are many different communication styles, yet only one that tends to yield the results we are seeking. Learning to express your primary feelings and needs, clearly, calmly, and with good eye contact is what assertive communication is all about.

Good communication skills allows us to deliver the message we want to deliver, while respecting our children (and others), listening to them and growing in our understanding of each other. Assertive communication provides us with the means to accomplish this.

Good communication skills are also an essential ingredient to better parenting practices because poor communication causes untold emotional hurt, misunderstandings, and conflict. Words are powerful, but the actual message we convey is even more powerful and often determines how our children (or others) respond to us and how we feel toward them.

Because communication is a two-way process, people with good communication skills are good at "receiving" messages from others as well as delivering them.

If you look at people in your life and at your own behavior, you may discover certain patterns of communication. Some patterns are negative and harmful while others are positive and productive.

Frequently individuals with poor parenting skills use harmful ways of communicating to their children and others. It is harmful in the sense that it disrupts relationships and usually does not accomplish the goals that are intended.

Assertive communication, on the other hand, is a much more effective way to get what you want and what you need without the negative consequences. In short, the development of assertive communication skills will work for you by making you a more effective and less stressed person.

Let's start by looking at the harmful patterns first and then at the assertive remedies that we have found really work for many class participants.

Harmful Communication Styles

Harmful communication patterns impact not only your children; they are also what predict divorce and partner conflict.

Let's review some of these patterns:

Harmful Pattern #1 – Avoidance

In marital research this is also called "stonewalling." Basically, it means being emotionally unavailable—cutting yourself off emotionally from the person you have an issue with. It can also mean not dealing with an issue by changing the topic, ignoring the other when they speak to you, or doing something else (like watching television) when your child/partner tries to discuss important things with you.

Example: Stacy and Bill were married for twenty years and had a thirteen-year-old daughter. At times the daughter would have meltdowns over a minor event. Bill could not cope with his daughter's behavior when this occurred. For weeks afterward, he would not talk to her. He basically ignored her despite his daughter's apologies and numerous attempts to emotionally connect with him.

Why do you think this is a harmful communication pattern?

_____

_____

_____

Harmful Pattern #2 – Criticism

Being overly critical toward our children or others is a harmful communication pattern because it puts them on the defensive and causes them to have negative feelings toward you. It is another communication pattern that predicts divorce—especially if it occurs with married women.

Does this mean we can never complain about things or let people know we are dissatisfied with them or their behavior? Of course not. But to communicate effectively, we need to complain in a certain way. A complaint is a specific statement of anger, distress, displeasure, or other negativity. Criticism involves attacking someone's personality or character, rather than a specific behavior. In relationships, a criticism takes a complaint and adds blame. It *feels* like you as a person is being attacked or judged by the other person.

The fact is, most people, especially children, cannot deal with too much criticism over a long period of time. Unfortunately, often highly critical parents don't see themselves that way. Rather they truly think they are "helping" their children in some way by constantly pointing out defects in his/her character and inadequacies.

Yet, constant, unfair, or high-volume criticism starts to just *feel bad* after awhile and erodes self-esteem as well as positive feelings towards your children and others in your life.

Do you think you may be critical of your children? How?

_____

_____

_____

Harmful Pattern #3 – Passive-Aggression

The passive-aggressive pattern is a harmful, covert way of communicating angry feelings, but indirectly, and it is sometimes without you knowing that you are doing it! Instead of confronting them head-on, it is a way of getting back at people without telling them why.

Often, the passive-aggressive communicator is trying to manipulate you or some situation in an underhanded way.

For instance, we might make a joke at someone else's expense. Or, we might make sarcastic remarks which communicate hostility or other negative feelings that we have.

The passive-aggressive communicator may also sabotage us, or our efforts, but in a way that it is difficult to prove that is what they are doing. When confronted, they will often deny that they are angry toward you or that they are doing anything to harm you.

Examples of harmful, passive-aggressive behaviors:
  * Making a cruel or unkind comment and saying you were just joking
  * Clamming up and not talking to your child because you are angry
  * Promising your child something and then "forgetting" that you promised it
  * Making negative comments about the other parent to/or within earshot your child
  * Arguing for the sake of arguing to escape dealing with the real issue.
  * Blaming your child for something that is not his/her fault

What are some other examples of passive-aggressive communicating?

_____
_____
_____

Harmful Pattern #4 – Aggression

A certain amount of aggression in some situations is acceptable, but some people consistently charge around to get what they want—in a way that is extremely harmful to good communication. Overly aggressive people like to have things their way and often express feelings in a way that punishes or intimidates (scares) their children and others.

Aggressive people tend to communicate by getting "in your face." They get too close to you, or stand while you are seated so they can dominate you. Often, they relate to us in a loud voice. They may gesture wildly. You may feel scolded or intimidated. They may give you orders with no thought for your feelings.

Children can very easily feel intimidated or fearful when a parent has an aggressive style of communication. The power, age and size differential between children and parents needs to be calculated into your communication with them. Add to that an aggressive communication style and an angry demeanor, language or conduct, and a child will most likely feel overwhelmed with feelings of fear or anger. They will not be able to take in what you are trying to communicate. This may lead them to shut down emotionally, to become resentful and may have a negative impact on your relationship with your child. And, whenever parents are out of control, yelling or overly aggressive in their communication style, the message the parent is trying to convey to their child is usually not received.

Describe a time when you have been aggressive in your behavior toward your children.

_____
_____
_____

Have you ever threatened your child in a way that caused bad feelings? Explain:

_____
_____
_____

Harmful Pattern #5 – Defensiveness
Defensiveness is a communication style that people use to emotionally protect themselves, rather than to openly listen to others or honestly express their feelings. Defensive people are not able to accept criticism from others, especially intimate partners, and therefore is another predictor of marital divorce. Defensive people put up a wall around themselves which prevents them from being able to take personal responsibility for conflict or problems with others. Defensive people are not open to feedback from others and are not open to changing or improving themselves. They see no need to change themselves. They take criticism very personally and are easily offended by even mild criticism or suggestions by others. They are emotionally fragile and don't want to hear things that don't "fit" their view of how things are.

Do you know of anyone who is defensive? How do they act?

_____
_____
_____

What challenges have you found in relating to such a person?

_____
_____
_____

Can you accept an honest criticism from your children without becoming defensive? What is an example when you accepted criticism from them?

You can be assured your children will know and press all your buttons It is important for you to acknowledge your vulnerability to that and not become defensive.

Harmful Pattern #6 – Contempt

Contempt is a communication style of regarding someone or something as inferior or less-than. In effect, we look down on them. Even worse, sometimes it means treating others with scorn as if we regard them as worthless.

When we are treated with contempt by others we feel despised, dishonored, or disgraced. Contempt has no place in healthy parent/child relationships. Making a child feel worthless or stupid are forms of child abuse and the result is serious emotional harm. Our children need to feel loved, honored and valued in order to grow to become emotionally healthy adults.

Some common contemptuous behaviors towards your child include:
  • Name-calling, swearing, or disrespecting your child
  • Denying the importance of your child's feelings
  • Saying hurtful, mean-spirited things
  • Any type of abuse or intentional neglect
  • Humiliating or ridiculing your children
  • Humiliating or ridiculing your partner, or ex, in front of your children

The Assertive Communicator

What is assertive communication?

It is a way to communicate so that you convey your rights in a good way. Assertive communication helps people clearly explain their wants, needs, and feelings to other people. It is a way of getting things that you want without violating or offending others' rights or having to walk away without getting what you want. Communicating assertively to your children not only establishes your authority as a parent, but also models and equips the child to assert his needs and wants in an appropriate manner.

Assertive people tell others what they want and need clearly. They have a knack for saying the correct thing at the correct time.

Assertive communication skills are the antidote to harmful and destructive communication patterns.

There are six steps to assertive communication. Each of these steps is remedy to the harmful communication patterns that we just discussed.

Assertive Remedy #1 – Send Clear Messages
Assertive communicators send clear messages, making sure that the message received is the message sent. With children, it is important to use words they understand, speak calmly and slowly, look them in the eye and avoid vagueness. Clear messages let children know what you think and feel and what you expect from them. For example, asking your four year old to clean his room may too be vague for him to know exactly what you want him to do. Be specific with your requests. In the example above, specific language might include "Your toys belong in the bin", "Put your dirty clothes in the hamper," etc.

Research shows that about 80% of the "message" communicated is done without words through "non-verbal" behavior. If your words say one thing, but your body language says something else, the listener may be quite confused. It's not always what you say, but how you say it that people respond to. Pay close attention to:

- Facial expressions
- Eye contact
- Posture (how you stand)
- Hand and arm movement
- Tone of voice

What are some ways that "tone of voice" can influence your communication with your child?

_____
_____
_____

Why is eye contact important?

_____
_____
_____

As opposed to speaking with adults, in what ways do you adapt your body language when speaking with your child, especially a young one?

_____
_____
_____

Respectful Communication
Modeling effective, respectful communication skills in all aspects of your life teaches children good communication skills. As parents, unfortunately, sometimes we communicate more respectfully with others than we do to our own children. Staying "in charge" as a parent never means speaking disrespectfully to our children. When having serious discussions or disciplining, you are actually more effective when you stay calm and treat your children with respect.

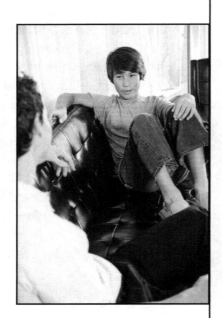

Assertive remedy #2 – Learn How to Listen

Assertive people have developed their listening skills. As you may have noticed, most people do not have very good listening skills. Listening is the most important part of effective communication. In fact, rather than really listening to you, many people unfortunately listen with their answer running—meaning that they are thinking of a response rather than listening deeply to what you are saying.

Hearing is done with our ears while listening is done with our heart. Listening is an active process. The listener must take an active role in the communication process. We as parents often need to say less and listen more. Are you really listening to your children? Practice listening to your child with an open mind and heart.

Children communicate in a variety of different ways. As parents we need to become adept at understanding how they communicate, the deeper message they may be conveying, the underlying need they are trying to express and learn how to respond appropriately. For example, we have all seen young children claim that they are not tired, but knowing them you can see that their body language is saying the exact opposite -they desperately need to get some rest, quiet time or go to sleep, no matter how much they protest.

It is that same type of awareness that we need to have when we are communicating with our children. What are they really communicating to us? Are they asking us to set limits, comfort them, reassure them, protect them, or guide them through a difficult experience?

It is important to realize that behavior is a language. Children may act out their needs, fears and struggles. Some children will demonstrate they are struggling by becoming more withdrawn, depressed, irritable and noncompliant. Other than verbally, what other ways does your child communicate to you?

_____

_____

_____

Is there an aspect of your child's behavior that is communicating something of which you should be concerned?

_____

_____

_____

Assertive Remedy #3 – Express Complaints Respectfully

Words have tremendous power to determine how other people experience us and how they respond to us. Expressing your complaints effectively requires different approaches based on whether you are dealing with a younger or older child.

Young Children

Too much wordiness can overwhelm and confuse young children. When trying to elicit or stop a behavior from your children, using words sparingly can help to ensure that the words spoken are understood.

Although often well intentioned, when guiding or disciplining young children, giving detailed explanations as to your reasons may actually be counterproductive and undermine your authority as a parent. You *do* know what is best for your child. You do not need to defend your reasons. Keep in mind, that your child will not appreciate any denial of their desires, no matter what logical reason you give them! In addition, always giving explanations can lead to opening the window for your children to debate your reasoning. And they are very good at that! Who hasn't heard a child's response to a mother's denial of their request for something because mommy has "no money" by stating emphatically, "Go to the bank and get more money"?

The key here is not about refusing explanations, because it helps children to begin to grasp the concept that rules are not made arbitrarily, but understanding that you do not have to defend your reasons, especially to young children. And when you do, the younger the child, the briefer the explanation should be.

As your child matures explaining why you have the rules and consequences that you do respects their growing intellectual and emotional maturity and independence. And as they enter adolescence negotiating with them on certain issues is a critical tool in teaching them how to solve problems and shows respect for their growing autonomy.

Using the Magical Formula- for older children, adolescents and adults

Parents with good assertive communication skills focus on the problem behavior (and not the character of the child or co-parent), stick to the point, don't use labels, and make "I" statements rather than "you" statements. The process to do this can be put into this formula:

I feel …describe the feeling you are having.
When you…describe the behavior that bothers you
Because…describe how the behavior affects you
I need…how you are requesting the person to change

Example # 1: Your teenager was supposed to be home at 7 p.m., but does not show up until 7:30 p.m.—with no phone call. Try communicating your justifiable complaint in the following way:

"I **feel** (angry, afraid) **when you** (don't phone when you are going to be late) **because** (I worry about you). I **need** you (to be more considerate of my feelings)."

Example # 2: You decide to take your preteen daughter clothes shopping. She becomes argumentative and disrespectful when you do not buy her a top because it is too revealing. Using the formula in this situation might sound like this:

"I **feel** disrespected **when you** speak rudely to me **because** I took the time and money to take you shopping. I **need** you to be respectful to me, even when you disagree with me on what you think is appropriate."

Example # 3: When your ex-partner drops the kids off 45 minutes late when you told them you were going to take them to the movies. You assert your position by stating:

"I **feel** irritated **when you** drop the kids off 45 minutes later than we agreed **because** it makes me think you don't respect the rules we've made. I **need** you to be on time when you drop the kids off to see me."

Does this formula work every time? Of course not. But, it does work a high percentage of the time and it should always be tried first before communicating the same complaint in an angry way. The "formula" when used correctly can convey a dissatisfaction or problem in a way that makes it a complaint and *not a criticism*. This often allows your child or other person to "hear" you without getting defensive or feeling attacked.

You asserted your message and your child or co-parent is defensive—maybe outraged. What do you do next? The following are steps to take when dealing with this kind of situation.

(1) Take the time to prepare your assertion calmly and sensitively.
(2) Offer the message. Do not hurl it.
(3) Use the silence as the initial response to the defensive reaction. Listen to the response and take time to consider yours.
(4) Actively listen. This reassures them that you are trying to understand what they are trying to say.
(5) Always keep focused on respecting your child (or co-parent), while staying firm with your position.

Communicating your Real Emotions
To manage difficult feelings as parents, it is important to recognize what the underlying emotions are and to communicate these emotions to our children.

For instance, a common underlying emotion of anger is fear. Often we show anger when in fact we are scared of something. Let's say your young child opens the car door while you are driving. Underneath, you are terrified of the possible consequences, but you express only anger and outrage at your child for opening the door. Only expressing the anger will not help your child understand the underlying concern. What a different response you might get from your child if you express your concern for his safety, yours and others, instead of only the outburst of anger.

Or, you may get angry at your child because he gets poor grades in school and he has the ability to do better. Expressing only the frustration is not as helpful as sharing the underlying emotion and ultimate concern for your child's future. Underlying emotions might be fear, sadness, disappointment, feeling inadequate as a parent or maybe even guilt over not being home more often to help your child with his schoolwork. Recognizing and communicating your underlying feelings and emotions is an important part of parenting because it helps you get to the real problem more effectively. It may drastically change how other people, including your children, respond to you.

Assertive Remedy #4 – Acknowledge Your Part in Conflicts

Being able to acknowledge our role in conflicts is important in maintaining healthy relationships with not only our children but also with our child's other parent. Good co-parenting skills is a process, involving two people who need to maintain a relationship with each other, and often over a long period of time.

When conflicts occur, it is natural to blame the other person (or your child) entirely for the problem, especially when we are angry and in a defensive mode. But, once we return to normal, the assertive communicator is able to accept some of the responsibility for the conflict. Taking some responsibility is an indication of emotional maturity and is an antidote or a remedy to defensiveness. You never win an emotional argument with facts, figures, or excessive logic.

Share an example of when you took some responsibility for a conflict you had between either your child's other parent or your child.

_____

_____

_____

Handling Conflicts
Parents "teach" their children how to handle conflict. For some of us, when we were young we learned healthy conflict management in our homes; for others, conflict was poorly handled and we not only failed to learn how to deal with it constructively, we also may have suffered the destructive or devastating results from poorly handled family conflict.

An exercise: What conflict resolution patterns did you learn in your family of origin?

_____

_____

_____

Often, conflicts become unmanageable because of the thoughts and emotions that get involved. Automatic thoughts, that is, those thoughts that have no real evidence to support them, are often the cause of unresolved conflicts. These thoughts can lead to incorrect assumptions about the situation or the persons involved in the conflict.

Useful Things to Say to Resolve Conflict
Our emotions can also get in the way of handling conflicts with our co-parent or our children. If you become embroiled in conflict, there may be times when you say or do things that are not appropriate or helpful. When that occurs, here are some things to say that will show you are taking some of the responsibility for the problem and respecting them.

- My reactions were too extreme. I'm sorry.
- Even though I still feel I was right about the issue, my reaction wasn't right, and I apologize for that.
- I really blew that one.
- Let me try again.
- I see your point. I know this isn't your fault.
- I never thought of things that way.
- I might be wrong here.
- I think your point of view makes sense.
- Let me start again in a softer way.

Assertive Remedy #5 – Give and Take Praise
Praise is an important part of assertive communication, both in terms of being able to give praise and take praise. Children need to receive praise from their parents. It improves their self-esteem and increases closeness.

Praise involves seeing the positives, what is right, and what you can honor and appreciate about your child (or their other parent or another person). This is opposed to parents who tend to see only what is wrong or negative, and then comment about the negatives. Praise is also a great reinforcement tool. When praising children, use it for conduct you consider praiseworthy and that you want to see continued. Complimenting your child too readily diminishes the impact of true praise.

What conduct is praiseworthy in your child?

_____

_____

_____

How do you praise your children?

_____

_____

_____

Do you compliment your child's other parent or your partner in front of your child? Complimenting your child's other parent affirms your child because your child views themselves as part of both parents. On the other hand, saying negative or insulting things about your child's other parent makes the child feel insecure about himself and puts your child in loyalty conflicts.

Assertive Remedy # 6 – Express Feelings Openly
Expressing feelings openly is a remedy for the harmful and destructive passive-aggressive communication style.

Many angry people "store" feelings or grievances they have toward others, but unfortunately, the negative feelings often do not go away, even if they are not expressed on the surface.

It is like putting the feelings in a bottle. You try to put the lid on tightly, but some of those suppressed feelings find a way to leak out. It is much better to deal with anger or resentment directly, before things get out of hand. If parents do not acknowledge their own frustration, they may explode later and cause harm to their children and experience personal regret as a result of it. If your children do not know you are upset with them, how can they change?

Why are some people so hesitant to be open and emotionally honest with others, especially people close to them? Some of the reasons psychologists commonly hear are:

- I don't want to hurt their feelings
- I'm afraid of what their reaction might be
- They might start being too honest toward me
- They might "emotionally" punish me in some way by withholding something I need
- It might undermine my authority as a parent

Despite these issues, it is important that you work at expressing your feelings because assertion is impossible until you learn to express your feelings. Learn to do this by practicing daily. Begin with small things. Express your feelings about something that happened. Once you become comfortable in expressing your feelings, you can take bigger risks.

Share a time when you were emotionally honest with your child or another person.

_____

_____

_____

Learning How to Communicate with Children

Communicating effectively with children often requires a different set of skills, strategies and understanding than in communicating with adults. Below are some of those that are important to keep in mind

when communicating with children.

Communication Dos and Dont's

- Listen actively.
- Make and keep eye contact.
- Look for the underlying messages in what your child is saying. What is the emotional tone or climate?
- Show respect for his ideas and feelings. Stay away from sarcasm, hurtful teasing, blaming, belittling, and fault-finding.
- Use "I" messages and avoid "you" messages and put-downs.
- Be honest.
- Be sensitive to the times and places that are good for talking. If your youngster comes home from school tired, give him some time to rest or have a snack before you communicate what may be on your mind. If you come home tired, take a rest yourself. Choose a quiet, private area in which to talk.
- Praise or reward your child from time to time when he shows good listening habits. He may be motivated to listen more carefully and follow through on what you are saying if his efforts are recognized.

If you and your youngster have ongoing problems with communication, ask your pediatrician for some guidance. He or she may suggest having your child evaluated for problems that may be interfering, such as language and attention deficits, or family issues. Your pediatrician might also be able to refer you and your child to a family counselor who can work out the difficulties that can improve your communication skills.

(American Academy of Pediatrics, 2004, p. 1)

Tool # 7
Discipline

For many of us the word discipline may bring up images of a stern, cold father figure or of being sent to the principal's office. For others, discipline may be a fuzzier concept because our own parents did not integrate a loving attitude when they disciplined us; they merely punished us when they became frustrated, frightened, angry or overwhelmed. They may not have seen the need to explain why they disciplined us, teach us positive alternative behaviors or affirm their love for us.

Purpose of Discipline

Understanding the purpose of discipline is essential in producing the desired result in your child and not punishing your child arbitrarily. "You discipline those under your supervision to correct, to help, to improve-not to punish." (Wooden and Jamison, 1997, p. 198) If the term discipline instantly leads to negative images, it may be helpful to replace the word discipline with the word *training*.

Training someone is *ongoing engagement to shape behavior*. It may be to teach a new behavior, reinforce desired conduct or unlearn an unproductive or maladaptive behavior.

Training a child shapes who they will become and involves every aspect of their development. Training children takes effort, time, patience, repetition and reinforcement. It also includes the reevaluation of the training's effectiveness. The training's ultimate goal is to *produce a benefit for the one being trained*, not to necessarily make life easier for the trainer! And what is the benefit of discipline, after all?

Discipline provides children with the inner controls to control their own behavior. It also teaches them to take responsibility for their own behavior, to learn to accept the authority of others, and to develop their conscience (Sachs, 2001, p. 210).

It is important for you to decide upon your general approach or principles of discipline. They will be your guide in responding appropriately to your child's conduct. Your style of parenting will undoubtedly influence your approach to discipline, as will your significant experiences with authority figures, your culture, religious beliefs, and your general outlook on life.

Your Discipline Approach (or Philosophy)

Waiting until your child misbehaves to determine what discipline approach to use will lead to overreactions, inconsistencies and fail to be effective in any meaningful training that discipline can provide. And when emotions are high we can easily act impulsively or out of control. We may also simply overreact to a child's *childish* conduct because *we* may be feeling overtired, stressed out or from a desire just to get the behavior to stop, not necessarily to train the child and teach him age appropriate, adaptive behavior.

Effective discipline is a conscious, rational response to your child's conduct. Discipline cannot be effective if it is inconsistent or irrational. It is important that you accept that you are responsible for the discipline you enact. Your child does not *make* you do anything. Remember your objective in any discipline: *to train your child in appropriate conduct while respecting their humanity and vulnerability.* Below are steps to developing a discipline approach.

First, decide what is acceptable and unacceptable general conduct from your children.

What are some behaviors that are unacceptable from your children?

_____
_____
_____

Second, make certain your children know your expectations. Don't assume they know.

Then, if your child, for example, hits his sibling you have already decided that this behavior is unacceptable and you know that a response from you is necessary. Now you will need to tailor the discipline to achieve your objective (training your child to have self-discipline, teaching appropriate ways to express anger or handle frustration, etc.), keeping in mind your child's age, maturity and any other developmental or health concerns. You do not need to find the exact consequence for each particular offense or misbehavior, but having a *consistent* general approach and a *consistent* implementation of it is critical in helping your child achieve self-discipline and learn how to function appropriately and effectively in the family and the outside world.

Third, decide before expected situations what an appropriate consequence for that behavior will be. Decide also what will not be used as a consequence.

What are some consequences that you use for misbehavior? What do you not use?

_____

This is important because it will help you to follow through, while respecting your child and yourself. It can also prevent you from over-reacting or acting inappropriately and possibly harmfully to your children. When giving the consequence it is always important to keep in mind your child's age, maturity, and other issues that may need consideration.

Fourth, make sure you explain to your child why you enacted the punishment and that you love him!

Discuss your discipline approach with any spouse/partner or co-parent. Coming to a consensus about this is vital in helping your child feel secure and become independent. It will also help your child to learn that there are consequences for their actions and that they are not the center of the universe!

Although some of us have supportive spouses or partners, others may be parenting alone or contending with an acrimonious co-parent or blended family. When it comes to discipline approaches, consistency from parents (or parent figures) concerning important issues is ideal. It is important, however, for you to act responsibly and circumspectly *no matter* what your family situation may be. This includes not overly focusing on areas that are beyond your control, like an ex-spouse who is not willing or able to have a rational conversation about important issues relating to your child.

What areas in your parenting situation are beyond your control?

_____

_____

_____

General Principles of Discipline

Below are some general principles of discipline (Komen and Myers, 2000, pp.93-94) that are important for you to think about and share, when possible, with any one that is parenting with you.

Have realistic expectations: What should you expect from a toddler or an infant? Should an 8 year old or a 14 year old do his homework without supervision? How do you know? It is critical that you *have realistic expectations that are communicated and understood by your child.* Know your child's capabilities and do not punish them for unrealistic expectations.

Discuss discipline philosophies with your partner or co-parent. Work as a parental team. Agree on the important issues and be willing to negotiate to come to basic agreements about major discipline issues. It is helpful to remember that you will both approach parenting with differing views because you were raised in different families, with different parenting styles, experiences, values, traditions, religions, and cultural influences. Your child needs for both of you to be on the same page when it comes to major discipline issues.

Make rules consistent, clear and reasonable. Make the consequence. consistent as well. For example, when your child argues with you about his established bed time, you give him an earlier bedtime the next night. If the same misconduct happens, have as consistent a consequence as possible. It is important to remember that young children have a very limited concept of time. Discipline should follow shortly after the inappropriate conduct whenever possible.

Rely when possible on natural and logical consequences. Natural consequences often make the best teachers. We often learn best when i costs us something. Think about what you learned as a child from the natural consequences of your actions.

For example, when I was a young child, my mother repeatedly told me not to run in the hallway. I didn't listen, ran into the door jam, cut my face and had to get stitches on my eyebrow. It taught me a painful lesson as to why my mom didn't want me to run in the hallway! I now have a deep respect for how slippery floor tiles can be!

What is an example of a natural consequence that has taught your child a valuable lesson?

_____

_____

_____

Do not use food or withhold affection as a means to discipline. These are critical to a child's health and wellbeing.

Positive feedback and encouragement are often the most powerful forms of shaping behavior. Whatever behavior is reinforced will continue. Share an example of when you have recently provided positive reinforcement, affirmation and/or encouragement to your child for a particular behavior.

_____

_____

_____

Do not physically harm your child. It is vital that you appreciate how easy it is to harm a small child. It is important to note, however, that it is not illegal in California to exercise reasonable and age appropriate spanking to the buttocks where there is no evidence of serious physical injury. A critical difference, among others, between child abuse and corporal punishment occurs when the child is harmed. For example, where a mark is left on a child, or when the child suffers physical harm, then that is not within the realm of acceptable corporal punishment.

It is vitally important, though, that if you plan to use physical forms of punishment, that you think this matter through carefully. If you choose to exercise limited, low impact corporal punishment, decide that you will never use it when you are feeling out of control. Reacting when your emotions are high can lead to using too much force, carry on for too long or dishonoring your child's precious body.

Understanding the difference between physical abuse and physical forms of discipline is critical if you choose to incorporate the latter in your discipline.

[In physical abuse, unlike physical forms of discipline, the following elements are present:

> • **Unpredictability.** The child never knows what is going to set the parent off. There are no clear boundaries or rules. The child is constantly walking on eggshells, never sure what behavior will trigger a physical assault.
> • **Lashing out in anger.** Physically abusive parents act out of anger and the desire to assert control, not the motivation to lovingly teach the child. The angrier the parent, the more intense the abuse.
> • **Using fear to control behavior.** Parents who are physically abusive may believe that their children need to fear them in order to behave, so they use physical abuse to "keep their child in line." However, what children are really learning is how to avoid being hit, not how to behave or grow as individuals. (Smith, M. and Segal, J. 2013, p. 3)]

Avoid implementing any punishment when your emotions are high. If you are very upset, first find something else to do that can release the energy from your frustration. After you have calmed down a bit, then discipline your child appropriately. Giving yourself a "time out" where you can regroup and be alone for a few minutes to think and gather your thoughts can be very helpful. This also teaches your children a way to deal appropriately with their own difficult feelings.

When you are upset, what can you do (or do you do) that creates a "pause" before you discipline so that you do not overreact, but instead respond appropriately to your child?

_____

_____

_____

Don't nag, scream, or resort to name calling. Avoid ridicule, sarcasm, or other indirect forms of communication. Remember words alone often do not motivate, action does.

Evaluate the effectiveness of your discipline. If something doesn't work, do something different! Is your effort producing the expected results? Are your expectations too high, unrealistic or does your approach need adaptation or a complete change? Evaluating your parenting does not mean beating yourself up over every imperfection. If you think something you are doing is not working, try something else!

What creative or alternative approaches have you tried when your first approach to solving a problem with your child did not produce the desired results?

_____

_____

_____

Judge the conduct, not your child's worth or essence. Be specific about the *conduct* that is problematic. Conduct should be judged; not the worth of your child. He has inherent worth because he is human. Watch your words- hurtful ones can cause immeasurable hurt and even lifelong pain and cannot be taken back.

Encourage children to express their feelings. This is often done verbally, but can also be accomplished via other means of communication such as writing, playing, physical activity, and creative expressions. Be ready and open to hear what they are expressing to you. At times it may be difficult or unpleasant for you, but listening to them when they are sharing their feelings with you is critical in helping them feel understood and to learn how to deal with their feelings appropriately.

Give children plenty of one on one attention. When you provide that, they don't have to act out negatively for your attention. Give kids lots of positive reinforcement.

Let children release their energy! Give very serious considerations before withholding physical activity or outside play as a punishment. Children need to release their energy and denying them that opportunity as a source of punishment will often lead to a more frustrated child.

Pick your battles carefully. What are some nonnegotiable areas concerning your child's behavior? (For example- substance abuse, dishonesty, disrespecting you as a parent) In what areas are you willing to do whatever it takes?

_____

_____

_____

What areas are important to you, but may not be absolutely *necessary* in raising a healthy child or achieving your ultimate goal for your child? For example, is a teen dyeing their hair really that big of a deal? Does it matter if your child does not want to do ballet or play in the school band? Is it that important that your daughter wear matching socks and barrettes for each outfit? Is an immaculate bedroom or perfect report card essential to your child's healthy growth and development?

What areas in your child's life (that you currently control) are not that *essential* to his growth and development? Are you ready to allow your child autonomy in that area? Relinquishing more and more of the decision making power to your child as they mature is a critical aspect of helping them learn to become more independent, to think for themselves and to learn from their mistakes. In what areas do you think your child may be ready to have more autonomy?

_____

_____

_____

Model, Model, Model! Model the conduct and attitude you want to see in your children.

In which areas are you a good role model and in which areas do you find room for improvement?

_____

_____

_____

Parenting Rules

Parents need to have proper expectations (rules) for their children, but sometimes parents have too many or not enough. This can lead to frustrated parents or unruly children. In an article Gibson (HealthyPlace. com, 2012) explains some parenting rules that provide a good foundation for children.

My basic rule of parenting is: There are no rules. The same thing will not work for everybody and things that work for nearly everybody won't always work. By experience, I've found that it is better to prevent problems than solve them. The following guidelines are as close to "rules" as I care to get.

1. Respect yourself. Be firm. Children will not respect a parent who has no self-respect. Be kind. Kids have tender feelings. Respect your child.
2. Have as few rules as possible for your kids. Don't have a rule you can't enforce or won't enforce. Choose your battles carefully.
3. Explain the rules before a child breaks one, not afterwards. Speak at the child's level (heads even) and make eye contact. Check for understanding by saying, "Tell me the rule." Don't ever ask, "Do you understand?"
4. Make the rules and set expectations appropriate to the child's age. Children becomes adults gradually, don't force it.
5. Avoid giving direct orders. There are better ways to win cooperation. Describe problems and let children tell themselves what to do. Instead of "Get your books off the table," try "Your books are on the table and the table needs to be set

for dinner."

6. Give children a choice when they misbehave: Do you want to stop playing or leave the table? If no decision is made, make the decision for them.

7. Don't give a choice when one doesn't exist. Avoid "okay." The word "okay?" at the end of a sentence tells the child he HAS a choice. "It's time for bed, Okay?" Don't ask "Would you like to take a bath now?" when it's bathtime. Announce, "Bath time!"

8. Don't give unlimited choices. "What do you want for breakfast?" will lead to hassles. "Do you want eggs or cereal?" Much better.

9. There are three things you can never force a child to do: eat, sleep, and potty. If you try, you will lose. Children win if they engage parents in a battle. You can't force a child to eat but you can make certain he comes to the table hungry. Separate bedtime from sleeptime. Keep children in bed at bedtime but they can choose to sleep or not. If you force a child to go to the potty, watch out for "revenge accidents" later.

10. Catch a child being good. What you notice you get more of.

11. Don't act like a child did something on purpose when it was an accident. Mistakes are not the same as faults. Teach how to make restitution, make amends, or sincerely apologize. These are life skills.

12. Avoid the following questions: Did you do it? (Did you see me?) Why did you do this? (don't know) or What happened? (Let's see, lamp broken on floor -- parents don't get it... parents not very bright). These questions teach a child to lie. Instead, state the problem and serve up the consequences.

13. Stay out of sibling arguments. You can never be the referee. Both kids will turn on you. [See section on sibling rivalry for a thorough discussion.]

14. Don't protect children from the consequences of their actions. If the logical consequences are reasonable in the first place, enforce them. If the natural consequences aren't dangerous, let them happen. Don't accept promises or only remorse thinking they won't do it again. They will learn to be manipulative. Consequences teach the lesson, not words. Yes, they will suffer. This is part of learning.

15. Avoid severe punishment. Logical or natural consequences teach the appropriate behavior AND responsibility for one's actions. Cruel punishment teaches revenge.

16. Give children your attention and your time. They can't live without it. Trust your instincts. When you love from the heart, you can't go too far wrong. Children are very forgiving.

Which rules are you currently using?

_____

_____

_____

Are there any that you would like to use that you are not currently using?

_____

_____

_____

Gain Compliance with Effective Consequences

Rules have no power unless there is a consequence for disobeying the rule. Below are tips on using consequences to gain compliance from your children (Keith, n.d.).

> **1. Give one reminder.** Say, what did I ask you to do? If your child responds correctly, say, "Good. Now do it". If she gives you that well-known blank stare, then get her full attention and tell her one more time, being very specific and firm.
> **2. Give one warning.** Now is the time to tell the child what the consequence for non-compliance will be.
> **3. Notice when your child does what you asked and praise her.** If she doesn't comply, implement the consequence immediately. Good consequences should be brief and related to the misbehavior.

Boundaries and Good Parenting

Boundaries are clear lines of behavior that parents determine and children know they are not to cross. Despite protests to the contrary, children need and want boundaries. It helps them to feel safe. Having parameters and limits for our children provides them with a critical sense of comfort and security.

Boundaries are all about freedom and recognizing when these freedoms have been crossed. Boundaries give us a framework in which to negotiate life events. Recognizing and acting when our boundaries have been crossed will protect our freedom. Boundaries lead to winning relationships for both parties. By building foundations based on mutual trust, love, and respect we can expect our children to grow up more tolerant and with a mature character. Simply put, boundaries simplify life (Randel & Randel, n.d, p.2).

Here are a few examples of children who lack boundaries (p.1):

> 1. Little Johnny walks right into his parent's bedroom whenever he wants. It does not matter if the door was open or closed.
> 2. Twelve year-old Steve frequently changes the channel on

the television. It does not matter if anyone was watching a show or not.

3. Susie blames others for her mistakes.

4. It always seems to be her teacher's fault, brother's fault, or a friend's fault when something does not go right.

5. Marie is uncomfortable with how her boyfriend treats her and pressures her for sex. She keeps dating him because she questions who else would want to date her.

Without boundaries children will have problems in relationships, school, and life. Many times addictive behavior can be traced to lack of boundaries. Here are a few results that can occur: (p.1)

1. Children can have controlling behavior.

2. Children can be motivated by guilt or anger.

3. Without firm boundaries, children are more likely to follow their peer groups. For example, by making unwise choices on sexual activity, drinking, or driving.

4. Children do not own their own behavior or consequences, which can lead to a life of turmoil.

5. Children may allow others to think for them.

6. They may allow someone else to define what his or her abilities will be. This denies their maximum potential.

7. When someone has weak boundaries, they pick up other's feelings.

8. Weak boundaries may make it hard to tell where we end and another person begins.

Another way to think about the concept of boundaries and how necessary it is to healthy development is to understand the role of sonar in dolphins. Dolphins rely on their sonar to detect conditions, objects, and predators in their environment so that they can navigate their environment safely. Without that sonar and its feedback, they would not be able to survive for long in their environment.

Boundaries, like sonar, provide a similar function for children. They let children know where the limits are, what your expectations are and how to behave. If they push (test) a boundary, there should be a response, just like the sonar does in a dolphin's world.
Expect boundaries to be tested. Your feedback from that testing needs to reinforce the boundary. The more consistent you are at reinforcing the boundary, the less often your child will need to test it.

When setting boundaries, it's important to keep in mind the following:

Boundaries should be reasonable, age appropriate, and *always* consistent. If there is no consistency, there is no boundary. Boundaries need to be thought through, discussed, and enforced jointly by both parents.

Boundaries must be clearly defined and easily understood by the child. All children will test boundaries; it's a natural part of development. So long as the boundaries stay solid and consistent, the children will eventually and usually quickly stop testing them.

When a child has crossed the boundary line, there must be a reasonable and consistent consequence. *A boundary means nothing without a consequence if it is crossed.* And let's face it, if this lesson is not taught by the loving guidance of parents, life will teach a child this lesson in a much more severe way.

Consequences should reflect the severity of the inappropriate behavior. If it's a one time slip-up on a small offense such as interrupting, all that may be needed is a simple verbal reminder…"It's not polite to interrupt." If it's more serious or habitual, then the consequence must be memorable enough that the behavior won't be repeated.

All children yearn to feel safe and know what's expected of them. Giving your child the means to do this through the establishing of boundaries will help them have a secure and well-adjusted life- a life which can bring them positive interaction with their parents, friends, teachers, and most importantly themselves (McCullough, p.2-3).

Tips for Setting Boundaries
(Randel & Randel, n.d. p 1-2)

What is a parent to do? Many times we hinder our children from developing boundaries. We must teach our children boundaries; they are not born with them.

Here are a few suggestions to help develop boundaries:

1. Recognize and respect the child's boundaries. For example, knock on their closed bedroom door instead of just walking in.
2. Set your own boundaries and have consequences for crossing them.
3. Avoid controlling the child.
4. Give two choices; this helps our children learn decision-making skills.
5. When you recognize that boundaries need to be set, do it clearly, do it without anger, and use as few words as possible.
6. We need to say what hurts us and what feels good.
7. It may be difficult to set a boundary. You may feel afraid, ashamed, or nervous, that's okay, do it anyway.

In addition, never forget the powerful teacher that your own life is to your children.

How are you modeling boundaries in your own life?

_____

_____

_____

Do you know and express what your limits are, both emotionally and physically? Give an example.

_____

_____

_____

Do you have your own opinions and do you let your children have their own? Explain.

_____

_____

_____

Do you take responsibility for your mistakes? Give an example.

_____

_____

_____

Setting boundaries is *all about taking care of ourselves*. Other benefits include:

1. We will learn to value, trust, and listen to ourselves.
2. Boundaries are also the key to having a loving relationship.
3. Boundaries will help us with our personal growth.
4. We will learn to listen to ourselves (trusting our intuition). We also will learn to respect and care for others and ourselves.

Tool # 8
Stress Management

While this section might seem generic to anyone, with or without children, we simply believe that good parenting and co-parenting skills must include the ability to manage stress more effectively. Being an effective parent IS stressful at times and dealing with an ex-partner may also be highly stressful. This next section is dedicated to learning more effective stress management techniques.

Dealing with Stress

In our profession, we often receive phone calls with the voice on the other end of the line saying something like, "Sir, I need help with my parenting, I think my wife is going to leave me if I don't do something about it." The voice continues, "I am a really nice guy, most of the time, but I just 'lost it' the other night and yelled at my kids calling them horrible things," he went on, "I don't know how to deal with all my stress as a parent, a husband, and an earner for this family, and I am becoming a monster…"

Our reply is often calming, as we know that learning stress management techniques, in conjunction with other skills, can greatly reduce one's level of anger, anxiety, and stress and can bring out the good parent or co-parent we know we can be.

As a parent we may be at our wits end with the constant crying of an infant, a toddler's temper tantrums or a teenager's defiant attitude. Stress and anger tend to go hand in hand. The higher one's stress level, the easier it is to allow our anger to get out of control. Participants of this class have often said they don't always know what causes their stress. The creation of stress is a simple equation. Stress is created when we have *more demands than resources to meet those demands.* For example, if in the morning you only have 15 minutes to let the dog out, get yourself dressed, put gas in the car, and drive your children to school in heavy traffic, this can create stress. Learning stress management techniques is an effective way to reduce the physical, behavioral, and emotional symptoms caused by stress. Managing our stress is also key in being an effective parent.

One of the major challenges of living and thriving in current times is managing our stress levels in a complex world with many demands and expectations. Small daily hassles such as making sure our children's homework is done or getting them to practice on time can add greatly to our level of stress. We can also feel stressed over much larger concerns such as future terrorist attacks on our country or becoming disabled or ill.

Our stress also affects our children. Whether we are stressed over finances, marital and family problems, work issues, health concerns, excessive worries or chronic anger, *children feel our stress*. It is important that we deal with stress in a healthy manner, not only for our own wellbeing, but for own children's wellbeing and sense of security in their own lives. How does stress affect us?

Stress and Your Physical Health

The effect of stress on your health can be significant. People suffering from intense ongoing work or personal stress may develop cardiovascular problems, such as heart attacks or hardening of the arteries. Chronic stress can also take a toll on the immune system, making you more susceptible to colds and infections. According to recent research, stress can also ratchet up the immune response to detrimental levels, resulting in allergies, asthma, and autoimmune conditions.

Other stress-related medical illnesses include diabetes, colitis, chronic fatigue syndrome, fibromyalgia, eczema, and ulcers. New research amazingly shows that long-term unrelenting stress on mothers can damage the DNA of their immune-system cells in way that may speed up the aging process.

Stress and Your Mental Health

Stress also contributes directly or indirectly to many common mental health conditions. Probably the most common are anxiety and depressive disorders and problems. In one study, two-thirds of subjects who experienced a stressful situation had nearly six times the risk of developing depression within that month.

Anxiety disorders are extremely common and frequently brought on by work and personal stress. Common indications of anxiety disorders include irritability, inability to concentrate or relax, insomnia, and a sense of fear. Many times people also have physical symptoms with their anxiety including nausea, heart palpitations, muscle tension, sweating, hyperventilation, panic, and bowel disturbances.

Depression is a disorder of mood and emotions which has a strong stress component. Often depressed people do not realize they are depressed because they get used to feeling sad with little joy or capacity to experience life's pleasures. Resentment, anger, and irritability are commonly a part of depression. Depressed people often feel hopeless or helpless, feelings made worse by stressful events in their life which they have difficulty coping with.

What is Stress?

Stress is a bodily response to life demands, which are called stressors. This means that your body stresses whenever a demand or requirement is made of you, and you respond.

This definition highlights one of the most important things to know about stress and stressors: what may be extremely stressful to you may not affect other people at all because of your different bodily responses to the same "stressor."

You may have better resources to cope with bickering children, carpooling or dealing with homework than another parent. Another parent might experience more stress from the exact same experiences.

For a potential stressor to be a personal stressor we have to first perceive it or experience it as such. This involves both memory and emotion. According to many scientists, for us to perceive an event as stressful, we must first remember it or something like it, has caused us trouble in the past. These memories are stored in parts of our brain called the "limbic system." The human brain is particularly good at storing memories with strong emotional content.

Stressors Can Be External or Internal

Sometimes the potential stressor may originate outside of ourselves and other times the potential stressor may be within either our own bodies or minds.

External stressors include job demands, degree you can make your own decisions about your job or tasks, your physical environment (noise, air quality, etc), marital conflict, parenting challenges, daily commutes on the roadway, financial pressures, and excessive demands on your time.

Internal stressors can be physical (like fatigue or illness) or psychological. Psychological stressors include job dissatisfaction, having negative feelings about your life in general, or holding resentments toward others. Other examples of internal stresses include feeling inadequate or inferior to people around you, or having excessive worry about aspects of your life.

Stress May Be Positive

Stress can have many positive effects such as challenging us to perform at higher levels, motivating us, keeping us at our peak, and focusing our thoughts and behaviors to reach an important goal or objective. This is especially true if our stressors are "acute" – this means that they occur, our bodies respond, we successfully cope, and then we return to normal.

In fact, according to *The American Institute of Stress*, recent studies suggest that short bouts of stress actually increase your immune system's ability to ward off infections and promote wound healing.

However, if acute stressors occur too frequently or are too intense, we may lack the resources to deal with it. Under these circumstances, we may become overwhelmed and enter a state which some scientists are calling being "stressed-out" as opposed to just being "stressed"

Stressed vs. Stressed-Out

Why do we have undesirable results of stress when stressors in our life become too much for us? The function of the stress response, after all, is not to cause illness or problems for us. Rather, most scientists feel that the fight-or-flight response evolved with the objective of ensuring survival and safety.

When things are normal, our powerful stress-response system sharpens our attention and mobilizes our bodies to cope with life events that we perceive as threatening. We cope, our bodies return to normal, and we go on with our lives.

But if stress for us is chronic or overpowering, then our system becomes overwhelmed or derailed; our stress response causes problems for us – medical, emotional or behavioral problems. In short, we become "stressed-out" or overloaded. When this happens often enough, our smooth running and protective stress system runs amuck contributing to numerous diseases and disorders which affect our bodies, our minds, our emotions, and our behaviors.

In order to buffer the effects of stress, we need to learn how to manage it. Here's how:

Four Steps to Stress Management

Step 1 - Develop Stress Alert!
Step 2 - Make Life Changes
Step 3 - Adjust Mind-View
Step 4 - Apply Stress-Guard

Step 1 – Stress-Alert!
This means becoming aware that you are stressed out. Many people simply are not aware of how stressed out they actually are, or how stress may be affecting their health and their behavior. Learning to recognize the signs is the first step toward dealing with your stress.

Warning Signs that You May Be Stressed Out:

• Feeling depressed, edgy, guilty, tired
• Having headaches, stomachaches
• Trouble sleeping or eating
• Laughing or crying for no reason
• Blaming other people for bad things that happen to you
• Only seeing the down side of a situation
• Feeling like things that you used to enjoy aren't fun or are a burden
• Resenting other people or your responsibilities
• Muscle tension

What signs do you notice when you are stressed out?

_____
_____
_____

Step 2 – Make Life Changes to Reduce Your Stress Triggers
Some stresses in your life are changeable, but it takes effort and commitment to make those necessary life changes. The most common stresses in this category are those related to how you manage time, how you manage finances, how you deal with family and relationships, and the amount of "overload" you have in your daily life. Another changeable stress is the "match" between you and your job or occupation.

Eight Practical Tips for Reducing Stress Triggers:

(1) *Take time off* – Take a vacation or a long weekend. During the work day, take a short break to stretch. Walk, breathe slowly, take a day off and go to the beach, and relax.

(2) *Manage your time* – Set realistic goals and deadlines. Plan projects accordingly. Prioritize your tasks. Schedule difficult tasks for the time of day when you are most productive. Tackle easy tasks when you feel low on energy or motivation.

(3) *Set limits* – When necessary, learn to say "no" in a friendly, but firm manner.

(4) *Choose your battles wisely* – Don't rush to argue every time someone disagrees with you. Keep a cool head and avoid pointless arguments altogether.

(5) *Use calming skills* – Learn not to act on your first impulse. Give your anger time to subside. Anger needs to be expressed, but it is often wise to do something that takes your mind off the situation. The break allows you to compose yourself and respond to the anger in a more effective manner.

(6) *If appropriate, look for less stressful job options* – But first, ask yourself whether you have given your job a fair chance.

(7) *Take control of what you can* – Learn to let go of what you have no control over and control what you can. For example, if you're volunteering too much or have over-extended yourself, try cutting back on commitments that are not essential

(8) *Don't commit yourself to things you can't or don't want to do*—if you're already too busy, don't promise to decorate for the school dance. If you're tired and don't want to go out, tell your friends you'll go out another night. Being able to say no is not only empowering but also a way of taking care of yourself.

Step 3 – Adjust Your Mind-View
For a potential stress trigger to stress us out and affect us, it first has to be experienced or perceived as a stressor.

Here is an example to illustrate the point:
Imagine, if you will, that there is a lion on the other side of that closed door you see at the other end of this room. If I can convince you there is a lion there, and you hear the growling, smell the lion, and hear the scratching at the door, how are you going to respond?

Usual response: *"I would be afraid and try to figure out how to get out of here."*

And what would your body be doing?

Usual Response: *"My heart would be racing, my muscles would tense, I would be focused on escaping."*

Now, consider the following: In terms of your stress reaction to this scenario, does it really make any difference if the lion is really there or not?

What causes the stress reaction in you is:
(1) Your perception or belief that the lion is there – not the reality of the lion being there or not!

(2) Your memory of danger in a similar situation. Now I know that you may never have encountered a lion at your door before, but you certainly have had experiences with the unknown, or wild animals, or seen ferocious lions at a circus or at the zoo.

(3) An emotional reaction to the event, usually fear. The extent of this emotional reaction will be determined in part on how unpleasant or traumatic the original event was that you are remembering.

Many of the stress triggers in our life don't need to stress us out if we just change our perspective toward it or develop better resources to deal with it. For instance, if you developed the skills of a lion tamer, that lion out there wouldn't bother you at all!

Likewise, you can change your mindset toward many things in your life that will reduce your stress. Start by changing the conversation you have with yourself by trying the following self-statements to reduce your stress:

- Don't sweat the small stuff. And remember: It's all small stuff.
- I can deal with this; I have dealt with much more stress in the past.
- Will this be important five years from now or even next month?
- This does not have to be catastrophic; it is merely a blip in my existence.
- Tough times never last; tough people do.
- My anger is a signal. Time to talk to myself and to relax.
- It is impossible to control other people and situations. The only thing I can control is myself and how I express my feelings.
- If people criticize me, I can survive that. Nothing says that I have to be perfect.
- Sometimes the things that stress me are stupid and insignificant. (I can recognize that my feelings come from having old primary feelings restimulated.) It is OK to walk away from the conflict or problem.
- I am feeling stressed because I don't have the resources to deal with this situation right now. I don't need to berate myself or put myself down over it.

Applying these principals to your life, how could you reduce stress by having a different mind-view of a stressor?

_____
_____
_____

What have you told yourself that has been helpful when you are stressed out?

_____
_____
_____

Step 4. Keep a sense of balance by applying "Stress Guard"

Let's face it, some stressors are unavoidable and are a part of our life —at least for the time being. In this case, we should learn ways to lessen the effects of stress in order to minimize the damage. Stress-guards include improving your health through diet and exercise, relaxation or meditation techniques, sleeping better, and developing social support networks.

This may seem easier said than done, but it is imperative in order to deal with the stress of parenting while juggling the other demanding roles and responsibilities in our lives. Especially for single parents, balancing your own needs against the needs of your children will require more effort, but is even more critical.

Take a minute to assess which "Stress Guard" ways, below, you do well and which ones may require more of your attention.

Physical Health
This includes eating habits, exercise and sleep and also getting medical attention when necessary and abstaining from substance abuse and other physically damaging behaviors.

Exercise
We all know that exercise is good for us; its effects on stress and your health are considerable. For example, numerous studies have shown that simply walking is one of the best ways to prevent heart disease. Some of the most promising research has to do with the way exercise affects the brain. Running, for instance, appears to make humans smarter. Other aerobic activities such as jogging, swimming, biking, etc. for twenty minutes three times per week is helpful in reducing stress. Other types of exercise such as yoga have been shown to have profound impacts on reducing stress and improving wellbeing.

Diet
A healthy diet helps to stress-guard us in many ways. According to some scientists, when you feel threatened or pressured for a period of time, your body assumes that energy supplies are being drained. Your stress response kicks in automatically, not distinguishing between running away from a predator and getting ready to fight with your spouse.

As part of this process, your liver is signaled to convert energy into long-term storage. Your stress hormones then encourage food-seeking behavior, making sure that your supplies are replenished. In one of biology's ironies, stress makes us hungry. If we then make poor food choices, our stress responses are intensified in ways that can very quickly spin out of control. It is also important to avoid caffeine and to not cope with stress by using alcohol or drugs. If you are stressed out, caffeine is like throwing gasoline on a fire to put it out!

Sleep
Scientists know that sleep is a vitally important activity in the natural world, although the exact reasons for this are not yet known. Sleep deprivation qualifies as a stressor in the sense of making life miserable and in the sense of producing more "load" on us to cope with. Trying to maintain normal sleep/wake patterns can greatly aid our ability to cope with our world when we are awake.

Emotional Health

This means being emotionally balanced in meeting our own needs and those of our family. If our emotional tanks are empty or running low, we will have nothing positive to give our children.

Is your emotional health a priority in your life or do you find your emotional tank is often on empty? What do you think might be helpful in maintaining your emotional health?

_____

_____

_____

Social Support

Talking to your family or friends can help by giving you a chance to express your feelings. But problems in your social life or family can be the hardest to talk about. If you think you can't talk to your family or a friend, look for someone outside the situation like your priest or minister, a counselor or your family doctor.

On the other side of the coin, protect yourself from negative coworkers, relationships, or family members. Do not get caught up in other's negative thinking. They will only serve to rip off your peace of mind and positive energy. Take good care of yourself and learn to recognize whether a person will help you or hinder you. Include in your inner circle only positive and encouraging people who will not only be supportive but also hold you accountable to your new goals.

Maintain perspective and a sense of humor

Perspective and a sense of humor can be extremely helpful in stressful times as a parent. If you are unable to have a sense of humor about anything for several days in a row, your stress level may be too high. Even though children can be stressful, they can remind us of the majesty of life and the absolute wonder and joy of being alive. Life may not appear to have many light hearted moments during stressful periods. It may take a change of focus to see what is good, wonderful or humorous in yourself, your children and your life.

What is good, wonderful or humorous in yourself, your children and your life?

_____

_____

_____

As the "tone setters" in our homes, humor can be such an underused approach to a problem. So much of life with our children is not as terrible or life threatening as we can make it. A sense of humor can be very helpful in maintaining a healthy perspective. Sometimes thinking of telling a friend about a situation and conveying the absurdity or humor in it can be helpful.

My daughter, never the star athlete, was on her high school's Junior Varsity basketball team. It wasn't her favorite sport but during one game she actually made a basket! Unfortunately, it was for the other team! It is funny now, but at the time I was embarrassed that she didn't know the rules. Looking back on it, humor would have been the best response. In the scheme of her life (which didn't include seeking college scholarships for basketball), it really was incredibly insignificant. It can be so easy to lose our perspective with our children and sweat the small stuff.

Describe a situation where you did not keep a proper perspective on the significance of a particular event in your child's life.

_____
_____
_____

Describe an event with your child where instead of reacting in a stressful manner you used humor to maintain a balanced perspective.

_____
_____
_____

Spiritual Health

Although we all have different beliefs, it is important not to neglect that part of ourselves. Life with children can go at such a frenetic pace that we can easily overlook the deeper, meaningful aspects of life. Take the time to nurture and restore your soul, whatever that means for you. What are some ways that you nurture your soul?

_____
_____
_____

How do you help your child nurture his soul?

_____
_____
_____

Relaxation/Meditation

Much research shows that relaxation or meditation can greatly reduce our stress and put us into a "health envelope." Studies show you should meditate twice a day for 20 minutes to achieve this result. But, you can also learn to meditate at work or standing in line at the grocery store. The trick is to breath deeply and then to focus on your here-and-now body feelings, putting distracting thoughts out of your mind. It is amazing what even a two minute exercise can do to reduce your stress and make you feel better.

The ability to recognize how your body reacts to stressors in your life can be a powerful skill. Most people are more aware of the weather, the time of day, or their bank balance than they are of the tension in their own bodies.

Your body registers stress long before your conscious mind does. Muscle tension is your body's way of letting you know that you are under stress. Body awareness is the first step toward acknowledging and reducing stress.

Breathing exercises have been found to be effective in reducing stress as well as anxiety disorders, panic attacks, depression, muscle tension, irritability, headaches and fatigue.

Ten Tips to Reduce Stress

Circle the tips that you would like to try or that could use improvement in your life.

Tip #1
Take 40 deep slow breaths each day. Spread them evenly throughout your day to avoid hyperventilating. You can benefit from associating the deep breaths with some common work occurrence such as the telephone ringing or watching the clock.

Tip #2
Use regular relaxation periods for work breaks. Try fifteen to twenty minute periods of undisturbed time away from the phone and/or family. Commit to using this for four to six weeks to begin to see the benefits. Suggestion: Take a short walk.

Tip #3
Get regular exercise. Aerobic activities such as walking, jogging, swimming, biking, etc. for 20 minutes 3 times per week is helpful in reducing stress. It kicks off stress-reducing chemicals in your brain. Be sure to check with your doctor first if you have any health issues.

Tip #4
Eat sensibly. Avoid caffeine. Do not cope with stress by using alcohol or drugs.

Tip #5
Plan for growth in all aspects of your life, not just work and finance (i.e. family, relationships, spiritual interests, vacations, hobbies, etc.). At the end of your life, you will not wish that you had spent more time at the office or that you had made more money.

Tip #6
Positive attitudes really help. Choose to see difficulties as opportunities for growth.

Tip #7
Try to protect yourself from negative coworkers and relationships. Do not get caught up in other's negative thinking. They will only serve to rip off your peace of mind and positive energy. Take good care of yourself. Learn to recognize whether a person will help you or hinder you. Include in your inner circle only positive and encouraging people, who will hold you accountable to your new goals.

Tip #8
Remember that you cannot control all the people and situations that happen around you. The only one you can truly control is yourself and the way you respond to stressful people and situations.

Tip #9
Give sincere compliments freely and smile. Choose to look for the good things happening around you every day; you might be surprised at what you will find. Reflect regularly on the people and things in your life that you are grateful for. Being optimistic is a choice; you can choose to focus on what is right and good in your life.

Tip #10
Learn to really listen. It is the best communication technique that you can develop. It is the highest act of love that a person can do for another.

Parenting Stress

Being a good parent can be stressful. Anyone who has spent one whole day with their child can attest to that. Some of us may forget that and we can set ourselves up for frustration when we expect effective parenting to be easy. It may be at times, but not always, especially when we or our children are going through periods of change or stress.

Parenting, however, can be the most rewarding experience of our lives. Part of making it rewarding and manageable is finding healthy ways to manage the stress that parenting brings. What are some ways to ease the stress and fatigue of parenting?

Caring for Ourselves as Parents

Although we each have our individual needs, limitations and parenting challenges, a few basic concepts of caring for ourselves can provide relief and keep us energized, healthy and sane as parents.

1. Nurture Yourself
In order for anyone to give love and care to another person, the giver must have something to give! Nurturing yourself is absolutely necessary to be able to do the same for your children. Nurturing

yourself as a parent also models for your children how to be healthy adults when there are ever present demands for one's time and energy.

Nurturing yourself may initially include images of deep tissue massages or exotic vacations, but those are not essential to nurturing yourself. Anything that takes care of your needs and some of your wants in a caring, responsible and healthy way is nurturing. Specific examples include buying yourself that expensive cup of coffee, playing golf with friends, watching something relaxing on television, getting a manicure, planning a vacation, going to the gym, etc. Other ways to nurture yourself involve valuing your thoughts, opinions and feelings, saying no to a request for your time and energy and saying yes to an enjoyable activity.

What activities currently nurture you?

_____

_____

_____

2. **Nurture your Relationships** with your significant other and supportive friends and family. If you have a spouse or partner, it is critical to nurture that relationship.

"Making a living and raising your children may demand most of your energy but, you should set aside a little time to nurture one another as partners" (Komen and Myer, 2000, p. 16). That relationship is foundational to your family. How do you nurture that very significant relationship?

_____

_____

_____

As you share parenting tasks and responsibilities, don't forget to set aside time to have fun! It is important to "share some good times as well as the meaningful but exhausting tasks of parenthood" (p. 17).

If you have a spouse or partner, how are you having fun together?

_____

_____

_____

It is important that you spend time with people who make you feel valued and who value parenting. Taking the time to visit with friends and family can help you feel grounded and connected in an uncertain and challenging world. It can also help you maintain a proper perspective when you are going through a stressful period.

Finding supportive people is invaluable. Whether you find them in your circle of friends, family, church, workplace, neighborhood or community organization, parent support group or counselor, it is critical that you have a support system. As author Rich Buhler profoundly states, "The only thing harder than going through a difficult time in your life is going through it alone."

What supportive relationships do you currently have?

_____

_____

_____

3. Make your home a haven! Life brings many stressors, some that can overwhelm or drain us. During these times we all need a place where all outside life can stop, where we can catch our breath and unwind. We need a place where it is safe to be exactly who we are, accepted, and to know that life is good. Your children need that, too.

Creating a relaxed atmosphere at home nurtures our bodies, minds and souls. As parents, we create the haven (or hell) where we live and where our children learn about life. Although we would most likely agree that having maids, nannies, and personal chefs would make our lives less stressful, this has nothing to do with actually creating a loving home or reducing our levels of stress. It does, however, have everything to do with our attitude and attention. How we spend our resources, time and money reflect what we value. We can choose to make our homes places we want to be, where we can get refreshed and where our families feel valued and loved.

Our personalities, dispositions, values and beliefs help create our home environments. Just as young plants cannot thrive without the proper environment for optimum growth, children also need places to feel safe where they can explore who they are in the context of a healthy, nurturing family relationship. That same mindset needs to be in our homes as we are the architects of the "mood" of our homes.

Take the time to think about the rituals, decor, items, people, pets, etc. in your home that give you a good feeling about being home. What are some aspects of your home life that make you glad that you are home?

_____

_____

_____

Our children deserve to feel that home is a place where they belong and that provides them with a sense of security and safety.

In what ways is your home a haven for your children?

_____

_____

_____

Below are additional suggestions for dealing with the everyday pressures of parenting.

Tips for Dealing with the Everyday Pressures of Parenting

(Child Welfare League of America, n.d., p.1)

- Stop…take a time out to calm down, reflect.
- Go for a walk or run. Work off your frustration through exercise.
- If someone can watch the children. Get away…go outside, go in another room, give yourself a little time alone.
- Turn negative energy into something productive…clean house, do yard work, and tackle some other job you've been putting off.
- Tune out and turn on some music, watch television, or read a book until you are ready to deal with the problem
- Talk with someone else about your feelings…call a friend or helpline.
- Write your feelings down on paper.
- Don't let anger build and build. If your feelings don't go away, get help.

Parenting the Child with Special Needs

All parents are very familiar with the stress of raising children and parenting well, but there is unique set of challenges known only to parents of children with special needs. Parenting a child who has special needs can be an overwhelming experience for most parents.

The stressors are quite unique for each family based on the special need or disability the child has, the dynamics of the family, and the support and resources available, yet there are common challenges that parents of children with special needs often face.

- Grieving - most parents experience this when they realize their child has special needs
- Managing the stress that often comes with parenting a special needs child
- Learning to understand your child's needs
- Redefining success for your child
- Navigating social services, medical and educational bureaucracies
- Helping all members of the family understand the special needs of the child
- Understanding how to appropriately discipline your child
- Managing your limited time, resources, abilities and energy C

Of those listed above which ones might you need additional support?

_____

_____

_____

How do you meet the needs of your child with special needs while balancing your own and your family needs?

_____

_____

_____

In parenting you child with special needs it is essential to have support. Who is part of your "support team?"

_____

_____

_____

(Stephenson, 2011)

Children and Stress

Children experience stress during times of change or times of crisis. Being supportive to children during times of stress begins with knowing what is "normal" for your child. The best indicators of distress in children are changes in behavior not typical for the child.

Common Children's Reactions to Stress (Bright Horizons, n.d.)

- Bed-wetting
- Fear of the dark, monsters, or animals
- Clinging
- Whining
- Nightmares
- Toileting accidents, constipation
- Loss or increase of appetite
- Fear of being left alone; fear of strangers
- Confusion/indecision
- Testing behavior or refusal to be cooperative
- Nail biting or thumb sucking
- Irritability
- Loss of interest and poor concentration in school
- Withdrawal from peers
- Regressive behavior (reverting to past behaviors)
- Headaches or other physical complaints
- Increase or decrease in energy level
- Indifference
- Depression

Have you noticed any of these in your children? Which ones?

_____

_____

_____

But remember, not all behaviors or behavior changes will stem from the crisis or revisiting of a crisis. All the other aspects of life and development are marching on: adjusting to a new class or school, friends moving away or changing allegiances, parents worried about layoffs, or a teen not having a date all create personal stress.

There are many ways to be supportive and caring to your children when they are experiencing extreme stress. Here are a few:

Helping Children Cope with Stress: A Quick Summary

1. Be available.
2. Provide a peaceful household.
3. Listen, listen, and listen some more.
4. Be honest and answer their questions – at their level.
5. Respect differences in children – individual and age based.
6. Encourage consistency, everyday routines, and favorite rituals.
7. Make the environment safe for talking about feelings and thoughts.
8. Expect and allow for all kinds of emotion.
9. Give choices and be flexible – avoid power struggles.
10. Allow a lot of opportunities and different media for expression.
11. Encourage activity and play.
12. Support the child's friendships and social network.
13. Be a model as a human being.
14. Hug with permission.
15. Practice patience.
16. Support children – at their worst.
17. Expect behavior that is typical of a younger child.
18. Expect behavior that is beyond the child's years.
19. Live right – eat, rest, sleep.
20. Make bedtime special.
21. Resist overprotection.
22. Don't force talk and interaction.
23. Understand that playing is a way to grieve and sort through fears and confusion.
24. Attend to the physical symptoms.
25. Reassure the child that he or she is not alone.
26. Set limits on acceptable behavior, and enforce them.
27. Remember triggers that will cause distress.
28. Plan family time together.
29. Be available for help if needed.
30. Take care of yourself.

(Adapted from 35 Ways to Help a Grieving Child, The Dougy Center for Grieving Children, 1999. See Resources)

From the list above, which ones have you practiced to help your child during periods of extreme stress?

_____

_____

Which ones would you like to practice that you have not?

_____

_____

Children and Trauma

Some stress is very great and may be traumatic. Traumatic stress is the physical and emotional response to events that threatens the life or physical/psychological integrity of that person or of someone critically important to her. It produces physical and emotional reactions, including an overwhelming sense of terror, helplessness, horror and other physical sensations.

Traumatic stress may result from any of the following:

- Physical abuse
- Sexual abuse
- Emotional Abuse
- Neglect
- Natural disasters
- Terrorism
- Traumatic loss/grief
- Medical trauma
- Accidents
- Witnessing violence
- Violent victimization

Exposure to traumatic events may result in Post-Traumatic Stress Disorder (PTSD). The short and long term impact of any given traumatic event partly depend on the objective nature of the event and the individual's subjective response to it. It is important to note, however, that not every distressing event leads to traumatic stress and something that is traumatic for one may not be traumatic for another.

The impact that trauma has on a child varies due to many things including: seriousness of the trauma, child's proximity to the trauma, prior experiences of trauma, child's relationship to the victim(s), child's age, and developmental stage of child when trauma occurs.

Children may re-experience the traumatic event and may also show symptoms, such as:

- Physical symptoms such as stomach aches and headaches
- Problems falling or staying asleep
- Difficulty concentrating
- Being irritable, angry,
- Having more and stronger, emotional reactions
- Acting younger

(American Academy of Child and Adolescent Psychiatry, 2011) For more information on symptoms of PTSD in children, see Resources.

Trauma does not always require professional intervention, but to successfully deal with it will always require caring, supportive others

If your child has experienced trauma it is important to make certain your child has the support he/she needs to work through it and manage the normal, yet difficult feelings and other symptoms that may arise. If you think or know that your child has experienced trauma which is unresolved and your child needs more support than you can provide, reaching out to a professional is the kindest thing to do for your child. It is not a sign of weakness- it is sign of human limitation and deep concern for your child.

If trauma has occurred, the following are important to help a child successfully deal with it: availability of sensitive and supportive adults, ensuring the child feels safe, additional resources available and a child's resilience.

Resilience in children is theorized to be influenced by a child's own temperament, close relationship with at least one parent or other nurturing adult, social support outside the family, affirming ethnic and cultural identification, ability to engage in self-soothing behaviors, the ability to choose people who model pro-social behaviors, child's problem solving abilities and social competence. (Cynthia Crosson – Tower, 2008, p. 62-63).

Trauma can come from a variety of sources, and its effects on children and adults for that matter also vary depending on a variety of factors. Many people experience harsh events in their childhood. If not processed and resolved, however, they may create long lasting harmful effects on their mental and physical health and wellbeing.

Examples of experiences that can be traumatic to a child include, but are not limited to the following: (From Adverse Child Experience (ACE) Study- See Resources)

1) Having a parent/adult in household:
- swear, insult or humiliate the child often
- act in a way that makes the child fear that he might be physically hurt
- push, grab, slap or throw something at the child
- ever hit the child so hard that the child was injured

2) Having an adult or person 5 years older
- touch or fondle the child's body in a sexual way
- attempt to or actually have oral, anal or vaginal intercourse with the child

3) Child often or very often feeling:
- No one in the family loved the him/her or thought they were important or special
- Child's family didn't/look out for each other, felt close to each other, or support each other
- That there was not enough to eat, had to wear dirty clothes, and had no one to protect him/her

- That his/her parents were too drunk or high to care of him/her or take him/her to the doctor if needed

4) Parents ever separated or divorced

5) Child's mother or stepmother
- Often or very often pushed grabbed, slapped, or had something thrown at her
- Sometimes, often, or very often kicked, bitten, hit with a fist, or hit with something hard
- Ever repeatedly hit a least a few minutes or threatened with a gun or knife

6) Lived/living with anyone who is/was a problem drinker or alcoholic or who used street drugs

7) Lived/living with a person in the house who was depressed or mentally ill, or who attempted suicide

8) Had a household member go to prison

Has your child experience any of the experiences, above? Which ones

_____

_____

Having experienced traumatic events can have a profound impact on not only the child but also well into that child's adult life. According to a large scale study conducted by Kaiser Permanente on the effects of childhood trauma to adult health, the more traumatic experiences a child has experienced, the more likely he/she is to experience:

- Alcoholism, alcohol abuse,
- Chronic Obstructive Pulmonary Disease
- Depression
- Fetal death
- Poor health related quality of life, illicit drug use
- Ischemic heart disease
- Liver disease
- Risk for intimidate partner violence
- Multiple sexual partners
- Sexually transmitted diseases
- Smoking
- Obesity
- Suicide attempts
- Unintended pregnancies

The important thing to realize is that trauma does not "just go away'. In order to heal, it must be processed. If you think you or your child have unresolved trauma, obtaining professional help may be helpful i healing those wounds.

113

Tool # 9
Children and Divorce

Divorce can be very stressful, confusing, and sad for parents and children. Anger is also common in children when their parents are going through a divorce.

How you handle this very challenging time for you and your children will play a significant role in how your children deal with the loss of their intact family, adjust, and accept the new and changing family situations.

> There are many ways you can help your kids adjust to separation or divorce. Your patience, reassurance, and listening ear can minimize tension as children learn to cope with new circumstances. By providing routines kids can rely on, you remind children they can count on you for stability, structure, and care. And if you can maintain a working relationship with your ex, you can help kids avoid the stress that comes with watching parents in conflict. Such a transitional time can't be without some measure of hardship, but you can powerfully reduce your children's pain by making their well-being your top priority (Block, Kemp, and Smith, 2012).

What routines do you have for your children?

_____
_____
_____

How are you maintaining a working relationship with your ex?

_____
_____
_____

As challenging and painful as divorce can be for all members of family, it is may be especially difficult for children with special needs. Your child may have many additional and complex needs that need to be considered in determining what is in the best interest of the child. When dealing with custody determinations or modifications, more flexibility and cooperation from both parents is essential to ensure your child has the least amount of unnecessary changes. This may be extremely challenging for co-parents who are in a high conflict divorce or custody determination. If that is the case, professionals may be necessary to develop a workable solution for your child. (Epperson, 2008) G

Rules for Divorcing Parents

If divorce is the best or only solution, protect your children by following the Heins Rules for Divorcing Parents. Here are a few of them (Parentkidsright, n.d., p.1).

1. Never put the child in the middle! Assure the children they will never have to take sides-and mean what you say.
2. Never bad mouth the other parent. Always refer to your ex-spouse with respect when the children are present. "Your Daddy loves you very much," is better for the children to hear than" Your Daddy is a lousy cheapskate who never gave me enough money!"
3. Both parents must tell the child repeatedly that:
   • The divorce is NOT THE CHILD'S FAULT.
   • It is OK TO LOVE BOTH PARENTS
   • IT'S OK TO FEEL SAD AND ANGRY because the family is breaking up. There's no way that divorce-which has been referred to as "social surgery" can be painless. Encourage the children to express their feelings. If they don't talk about it ask them how it hurts and help them deal with the pain.
   • There's nothing to be ashamed about; the divorce is between the parents. Be sure to help the child tell others about the divorce. Sometimes children are embarrassed and don't know what words to use to tell their teacher or friends.
   • "You will always be taken care of" and "we both love you."
4. Let the child see where the non-custodial parent is going to live. The child needs to know that both parents will be safe and warm and have a place to live.
5. Help the child's life be as predictable as possible. Children need to know what will happen to them. If you are going to sell the house, tell them.
6. Keep lines of communication wide open so together you can always do what is in the best interest of the child.
7. Don't squabble in front of the children. Stay civil to each other and "talk nice" to each other. A matter of fact, even if the marriage is over, I recommend counseling. You must be able to communicate about the children post-divorce.
8. Never use the child to carry messages of your anger or grief back and forth.
9. Get counseling help for your child if the child has trouble in dealing with the divorce. Children of divorce may exhibit behaviors ranging from denial and indifference to depression, regression, anger, guilt, and problems at school. If these seem to be escalating, get help.

What rules, above, are you following?

_____

_____

Which ones need improvement?

_____

_____

Children and Divorce: Guidelines for Divorced Parents to Live By: Do's and Don'ts (Mc Ghee, n.d.)

The Do's:

- **Do love your child as much as possible.** Show them your love through words and actions.
- **Do tell your children the divorce is not their fault.** Tell your children this repeatedly, they need to hear it more than once. (See Resources)
- **Do reassure your children that they will be safe.** Let them know both parents will continue to provide for them to the best of their ability.
- **Do let your children know it is okay to love both mom and dad as they did before the divorce.** Let kids know the love they have for both parents doesn't have to change.
- **Do support your children's relationship with the other parent.** Inform the other parent of special events, school functions or extracurricular activities whenever possible.
- **Do listen to your children.** Honor their feelings without judging, fixing or trying to change how they feel. Remember, your children's feelings don't have to reflect your feelings.
- **Do let your children know it is okay to express those feelings.** Your child will need help learning safe and healthy ways to express their feelings. Be sure to provide them with appropriate options.
- **Do reinforce that children are members of two homes.** Children should not be made to feel guilty or as if they have to choose which is their "real" or "better" home.
- **Do help children feel like they have a home with both parents regardless of the amount of time spent with each parent.** Make sure children feel they have a place in each home that belongs to them, even if it is only a section of a room. Giving children the opportunity to offer input or add their own touches to their space can be helpful.
- **Do provide your children with discipline, as well as love.** Children still need parents to provide structure and limits, especially during difficult times.

Which of the *Do's* are you currently doing?

_____

_____

_____

Which ones do you need to improve or implement in your parenting?

_____

_____

The Don'ts

- **Don't badmouth, judge or criticize your child's other parent.** Children literally view themselves as half mom and half dad. Therefore when you attack the other parent you attack your child. This rule also applies to stepparents and other significant adults in your child's life.
- **Don't expose your children to divorce details.** Rarely is it ever in the best interest of children to be exposed to information regarding court matters, child support, financial concerns or intimate details regarding your divorce. Typically children feel very confused and caught in the middle when parents expose them to adult issues.
- **Don't use your children as messengers or spies.** Be responsible for finding some way to communicate with your ex-spouse.
- **Don't retaliate when the other parent says or does damaging things.** Retaliation or giving you children "your side of the story" continues the cycle of children feeling very confused and caught between mom and dad. Instead, choose to be supportive of your children by using statements such as "I am sorry you had to hear that" or "How do you feel when this happens?"
- **Don't make your child responsible for making adult decisions.** Children should not be placed in the position of deciding parenting schedules, where they will live or how to handle household matters.
- **Don't allow your children to become your best friends or confidants.** Children should not feel responsible for their parent's well-being. Make sure you develop a supportive network and find other caring adults to share your feelings with about the divorce.
- **Don't place blame when children ask why the divorce happened.** Children should not be placed in the position of judging or taking sides.
- **Don't withhold visitation if child support is unpaid or a fail to pay child support if the other parent is withholding visitation.** Both actions are illegal and are viewed as separate issues by the court.
- **Don't try to buy your child's love or out buy the other parent.** While children enjoy gifts, they will remember you for how you cherished them, not for the material things you bought them.
- **Don't lose your sense of humor.** It comes in handy during stressful times.

(Reprinted with permission.)

Which of the *Don'ts* are you currently doing?

_____

_____

Which ones do you need to improve or implement in your parenting?

_____

_____

Co-Parenting and Step Parenting

Co-Parenting

What is co-parenting? Co-Parenting simply means that a child has two parents not living in the same home that are raising him/her. In order do this successfully, parents act jointly in the best interest of the children, share parenting time, are both involved in decision-making and are able to communicate effectively with each other.

If formal co-parenting plans are part of the decree of dissolution, they can be legally enforced. Keep in mind that co-parenting plans can be changed as the child grows and his/her needs change, but this requires court approval.

The objective of any co-parenting plan or arrangement should be what is the best interest of the child. "Best interest of the child" is a key phrase in the law of all U.S states. The courts are mandated by the statutes to make custody decisions with this factor as its benchmark.

Co-parenting and Custody Decisions: Factors to Consider

In deciding who will have custody, the courts consider various factors. (Findlaw, n.d. p. 1) The overriding consideration is always the child's best interests, although that can be hard to determine. Often, the main factor is which parent has been the child's primary caretaker. If the children are old enough, the courts will take their preference into account in making a custody decision.

Although the "best interest" standard does vary from state to state, some factors are common in the best interest analysis used by the individual states, including:

- Wishes of the child (if old enough to capably express a reasonable preference)
- Mental and physical health of the parents
- Religion and/or cultural considerations
- Need for continuation of stable home environment
- Support and opportunity for interaction with members of extended family of either parent
- Interaction and interrelationship with other members of house hold
- Adjustment to school and community
- Age and sex of child

- Parental use of excessive discipline or emotional abuse; and
- Evidence of parental drug, alcohol or sex abuse.
  (See Resources to learn more about preparing a co-parenting plan how to get or change a court order and other resources to help you and your children through your separation and divorce.)

Successful Co-Parenting (Hirschfield, n.d.)

How parents negotiate their childrearing beliefs and their day-to-day shared parenting responsibilities is called co-parenting. When mothers and fathers can agree on parenting decisions, the positive benefits of co-parenting are seen. Mothers and fathers who agree on parenting issues and support each other's efforts create an environment that allows children to grow and thrive.

After a divorce or separation it may seem unthinkable to begin to build a new parenting relationship with an ex-spouse. But with effort, it can be done. Conflict between former partners is often inevitable; what is important is how the conflict is managed. Some possible sources of conflict are:

- Money
- Medical issues
- Religious/values education
- Education and/or career plans
- Holidays
- Recreation (sports, hobbies)
- Discipline

Keys to successful co-parenting

- Base your new relationship with your ex on basic business principles. Form a working relationship. How you feel about your ex is less important than how you act toward him/her.
- Respect your need for privacy and the other parent's too. The only information that needs to be shared between co-parents is that pertaining to their children.
- Each parent has the right to develop his/her own parenting styles. As long as no harm is being done, let your ex-spouse relate to your child as he/she sees fit.
- Acknowledge what your ex-spouse has to offer your child. Remember the qualities that first attracted you. Those qualities still exist and are available to your child.
- Make a serious effort to live up to the terms of the time sharing agreement.
- Tell the other parent in advance about necessary changes in plans
- Try to be reasonably flexible in "trading off" to accommodate each other's needs.
- Prepare your child in a positive way for each upcoming stay with the other parent.

- Do not conduct custody, visitation, or support discussions when you meet to transfer your child. Work on your problems with the other parent in private.
- Do not use your child as a confidant, messenger, bill collector, or spy.
- Listen to your child concerning problems with the other parent, but encourage your child to work out the problems with the other parent directly.

Which of the keys are you currently doing? Which ones do you need to work on?

_____

_____

_____

What your child needs to know:

- The child has not caused the divorce.
- Neither parent is rejecting the child.
- The child will still have a family, even though the parents will no longer be married to each other.
- Although the parent's feelings toward each other have changed, the parents' love for the child will go on forever.
- The parents will continue to take care of the child and provide for him/her.
- The parents should try to agree on a reasonable explanation to give the child on why they are getting a divorce. The child needs just enough information to explain the divorce. Too many details may be confusing.
- As soon as matters are settled, the child needs to know what things will stay the same and what things will change: which parent the child will live with and when he/she will see the other parent, where the child will live and go to school, when the child will see other family members (grandparents, aunts and uncles) and so on.
- Tell your child that it's OK to feel sad about the other parent's leaving or absence.
- Helping your child through the adjustments and difficulties of divorce means being in touch with their feelings of loss, guilt, powerlessness and fear.
- Stick to a daily routine with your child, similar at both houses whenever possible.
- Acknowledge that your child may wish to have you and your former partner get back together, but do not encourage or support this wish.
- Talk with your child honestly about changes or moves that will affect him/her before they occur.
- Support your child's need to visit with the other parent.
- Support your child's desire to love both parents. Tell your child that it's still OK to love both of you, even though you're no lon-

ger going to be married to each other.
- Don't try to use your child as your counselor or your source of emotional support. Seeing parents as needy and dependent on them may make a child feel very insecure. Find an adult who can fulfill those needs for you.
- Remind your child that his/her parents will still take care of him/her
- Show your child that you trust his/her ability to adapt to these changes.
- Promote relationships between your child and other safe, healthy and caring adults including extended family, friends and professionals.

Which of the statements, above, does your child know?

_____

_____

_____

What NOT to do

- Do not withhold visitations from the other parent.
- Do not use your child to spy on the other parent.
- Do not use your child as a pawn or bargaining chip in fighting over family property.
- Do not use your child as a go-between to resolve issues with your former partner.
- Do not speak negatively and angrily about your former spouse in front of your child.
- Do not compare your child with the other parent in a negative way.
- Do not argue with the other parent in front of the child.
- Do not use your child to pass on information and messages to the other parent.

(Reprinted with permission)

Make sure to take care of yourself. Depending on your circumstances, your own emotional and physical energy may be low. Find ways to take care of yourself so you can fully care for your children and deal with the stress and challenges that parenting and co-parenting bring. How are you taking care of yourself?

_____

_____

_____

General Guidelines for Co-parenting (Craig, 2012)

A co-parenting plan is a contract that you and the other adult agree on for set guidelines you will follow.

The reality, however, is that people change. Rules change, living situations change, and people move on to new relationships. The parenting plan addresses many of the pitfalls that come about to keep you out of court or conflict with the other parent. Because dividing time between adults consists of such trust with the other parent, this in a large way promotes some security that you agree on areas. The age of the child has a great bearing on how detailed you need to be. Young children NEED consistency between homes where older children are more adaptable, but may require more rules. Parenting Plans help future relationships because it allows the significant others in your present or future to read what you agreed on and you will be less prone to follow a different path than what you initially agreed on.

It would be very difficult for someone else to create the best parenting plan for each of you and your children. Co-parenting plans are created to meet the on-going co-parenting and family rules that should not end just because a relationship has ended or because there is conflict. You will find even "experts" can't agree on very important issues that are fundamental to co-parenting. You know your child better than anyone else and both parents know what direction they want to raise the child in.

Although you and your co-parent may not completely agree on all areas related to parenting, what is required from you is only a *willingness* to sort through the important issues. An important goal would be for you and your co-parent to be on the "same page" when it comes to *critical* issues.

Accepting that there will be areas where you simply *may not agree* is important to allow you to focus your energies on areas that are important to your child's development and well-being.

List a minor issue where you and your co-parent disagree?

_____
_____
_____

Is there a major area of parenting in which you and your co-parent are in great disagreement? What is that?

_____
_____
_____

In what areas are you and your co-parent in agreement?

_____
_____
_____

Deciding and keeping the best interests of your child in mind will be helpful in weeding out minor differences in parental preferences from important issues where compromise and a collaborative mindset are more beneficial. This may take a certain amount of "not getting your own way" and accepting that you are ultimately only responsible for your relationship with your child; the other parent is responsible for their relationship.

Share an example when you compromised or were flexible with your child's other parent about an issue related to your child?

_____

_____

_____

Tips for establishing a successful co-parenting relationships with your ex-spouse (McGhee, n.d. p. 1)

One of the most damaging aspects of divorce is parental conflict. Exposing children to conflict can:
- Place the children in loyalty conflicts
- Continue or escalate children's feelings of fear and insecurity
- Damage children's self-esteem and sense of identity
- Prolong short term reactions to divorce and keep children from successfully adjusting
- Contribute to the development of negative long term reactions
- Keep children feeling responsible for the divorce.

Despite the fact that your relationship as a married couple has ended, your roles as mom and dad will continue for a lifetime. Children function best when they are able to have a nurturing, supportive relationship with both parents. Below are some tips to help you parent with someone you could not be married to.

- **Avoid conflict in front of your children at all costs.** Often contact between parents initially is difficult and can be a breeding ground for open warfare. If you, or the other parent, are having difficulty avoiding conflict try to create other options that may decrease potential confrontations. Arrange for pickups or drop-offs take place in a neutral setting. Also, make sure children are not in listening range when telephone conversations are being held with the other parent. If necessary use written communication, voicemail, text messages or email to share information if your child is with the other parent.
- **Establish a business relationship with your ex which is focused on the best interest of your children.** Your relationship as husband and wife has ended; however, you both continue to have lifelong investment in the well-being of your children. Avoid conversations that address old issues, personal information or encourage conflict. If you are having difficulty separating your emotions from the situation or person, ask yourself how you would handle a similar situation with a fellow co-worker. Sometimes it may be helpful to think about how you would want the situation handled if the roles were reversed.

• **Change your expectations.** Following divorce, some parents try to control one another through resorting to manipulation, confrontation, and bad mouthing. Don't put energy into trying to control your ex or the situation. The most you can do is be the best parent you can be and strive to influence your children in a nurturing and supportive way.

• **Control your anger.** If you find yourself reacting to something your ex has said or done, find some way to distance yourself from your immediate response. Give yourself time to vent to a friend, sort through your feelings and cool off. Approach your ex at a later time once you have sorted through things. Instead of waging a personal attack, stay focused on addressing the issue. Also try utilizing negotiation tactics during times of disagreement.

• **Be supportive of the other parent's role in your child's life.** Remember just because your ex wasn't a good partner doesn't mean they can't be a good parent. Speak positively about the other parent to your children when possible. (If you can't, you are probably better off not saying anything.)

• **Resolve feelings and issues regarding your ex-spouse.** Find some way to address your issues related to divorce verses hanging onto the anger and hurt. Moving forward is important for both you and your children. If you are having difficulty, find some help.

• **Take responsibility for communicating with your child's other parent.** Inform the other parent of school functions, important details, extracurricular activities and special events whenever possible for your child's benefit.

• **When possible be flexible and willing to compromise.** Where children are concerned, plans are always subject to change. Be open to changes or agreements which serve your children's best interest. It also sets a good example for children when parents are willing to work things out.

Which of the tips, above, are you actively using or trying to implement?

_____

_____

_____

Tips for the less than Ideal Situations

Although you have no control over the choices you ex-spouse makes, you do have control over the choices you make. Below are some tips to keep in mind when situations are difficult or filled with conflict.

• **Keep discussions with your ex focused on the best interest of your children.** If your ex brings up old arguments or issues, don't get into a debate over who is right and who is wrong. Refocus the conversation on the issue at hand and stick to the task—parenting your children.

• **If face to face contact is too difficult, use email.** Email can be a good way to exchange ideas or information about the children and minimize conflict. Exchanging angry emails at each other will not help your children, though.

• **Don't retaliate when your ex launches a personal attack.** Even though it may be hard when your ex says or does something to push your buttons, take the high road and avoid reacting to your ex spouse's inappropriate behavior.

• **Find safe and healthy ways to vent/process your feelings.** Dealing with conflict can be draining. Make sure you are handling your feelings and that you have supportive outlets, as well as a supportive network.

• **Strive to provide your children with consistency and stability regardless of the other parent's actions.** Focus on what you can control, not what you can't. While you may not agree with the other parent's choices, children will still fare better if they have a loving stable relationship with at least one parent.

• **Don't get yourself worked up over the small stuff.** When emotions are running high it is easy for issues to become much bigger than they actually are. To gain perspective ask yourself, what difference will this make six months from now? A year?

• **Don't use drop-offs or pick-ups as a time to discuss information regarding the children.** Schedule mutually agreeable times to either talk over issues or choose to share information by email. Pick-ups and drop offs can be emotional times for children and parents.

(Reprinted with permission.)

If your children are living in two homes, you can help to make that less stressful for them by following these tips.

Two Homes: Tips for Parenting out of Two Homes
(McGhee, n.d., p 1)

• **Encourage a two home concept.** Children should feel they have a home with both Mom and Dad regardless of how much time is spent with either parent.

• **Be supportive of both homes.** Avoid judging or criticizing your child's home with the other parent. Comparing the two homes or trying to find fault with one home only leaves children feeling caught in the middle.

• **Establish structure for your children within your home.** In some divorce situations, parents work cooperatively to maintain the same rules for their children in each home. However, for a vast majority of families, agreeing on rules is difficult. What is most important is that children feel secure in the understanding that the adults are in charge and things are going to be okay. Children can adjust to the differences between two households when they know what to expect.

• **Be supportive of the other parent's role.** Whenever possible communicate with the other parent about the needs of your child (i.e. school events, medical appointments, birthday parties, extra-curricular activities, friends, etc.)

• **Let children know what to expect.** Many children (especially younger children) do not handle sudden change well. Help children feel more secure by giving them information about family plans. Sometimes items such as calendars outlined with information about where, when, and which parent a child will be with can decrease anxiety.

• **Keep birthdays, holidays and other important events special for your children.** Avoid getting into competition with your child's other parent over who will make a birthday the most special or who will buy the best presents. When possible, coordinate with your ex-spouse regarding gift giving and special activities so your child does not feel overwhelmed or conflicted.

• **Don't give gifts to children with strings attached.** Before giving your child a gift, think about how you will handle where that gift ends up. It is usually best to let children decide where a gift will live. If you want to give a child something that is meant specifically for your home, let your child know that up front. If a present is for their other home, talk with the other parent about the gift first.

Which of the tips, above, are you currently doing?

_____
_____
_____

And which tips do you need to improve?

_____
_____
_____

And, if you are the parent who does not have primary custody, the following tips can help your children in adjusting to the new arrangement.

Two Homes: Tips for the Non-Custodial Parent
(McGhee, n.d., p 2)

• **Help children feel physically connected to your home.** Provide children with a space for their things even if it is only a corner in a room. Sometimes having children help place pictures or give input about where things go can be helpful. This also lets children know they are an important part of your home.

• **Consider providing children with two sets of personal items, clothes, etc.** While it is not always economically feasible, when possible it may help children's adjustments if they are able to have what they need at both homes verses taking suitcases back and forth.

• **Avoid treating your child like a guest in your home.** Include

126

children in family activities such as doing the laundry, making dinner and cleaning up. You can also create new family rules or activities that allow you to enjoy time together.

• **Minimize distractions for children in making a positive transition between homes.** It may be helpful, especially with younger children, to develop some type of routine or ritual for transition times. It could be as simple as taking a walk together before going back to the other parent's home. Children usually have a greater sense of security and feel more in control when they know what to expect.

• **Let children know they are an important part of your home.** Quit often we pay little attention to how things change in our home on a day to day basis. However, for children, those changes we may view as small or insignificant can be a big deal. When children are not prepared for change it may throw them into sensory overload or contribute to them feeling insecure. Try to keep kids informed of changes that are taking place in your home. It will help them to feel connected.

(Reprinted with permission.)

Step Parenting and Step Families

Step families provide challenges for all family members, especially for children. It is important to understand both step family dynamics as well as the step family life cycle. Many divorcing and remarrying couples do not fully understand the impact their new marriage will have on their children. (Niolon, 2011, pp. 1-2) For information on this see Resources. In addition, there are key tasks in become a step family.

Key Tasks in Becoming a Stepfamily (Niolon, 2010, p. 3)
Step families must solve 4 basic tasks to survive:

1. Integration
• Integrating the stepfather/stepmother into the children's lives
• Integrating the step- family into the step-children's lives.
• Developing a shared vision of family life, which must include making a decision regarding how close the stepfather/ stepmother and child will be (i.e., buddies or closer, consultant or discipline partner with the biological parent?)

2. Creating a Satisfying Second Marriage
This entails taking care of each other, and separating from the first marriage. Happy second marriages help the parents live through the stress of the first two years. This also entails keeping ex-partners from interfering and creating additional stressors and maintaining old dysfunctional patterns. It is important to set rules about what responsibilities a stepmother/stepfather will have and accept

how this fits into his/her schedule, and under what conditioned he/she accepts additional responsibilities.

3. Managing Change in the Family

This is an especially difficult task to manage, since much of the change that step families must deal with comes from factors beyond their control. For example: visiting step-grandparents, rules imposed by ex-partners about parenting, children's development and changing needs, integration of non-custodial children, changing roles of parents and step-parents over time and the unpredictable results of mixing this many people into the step-family.

4. Creating Good Working Rules

This entails creating, trying, refining, rejecting, and finally agreeing on workable rules for handling the cast of peripheral characters (absent biological parents and step-parents, step-in-laws) that enter the family's life from time to time.

Which basic tasks have you accomplished, are working on, or are having problems with?

_____
_____
_____

Of the task that is most challenging at this time, how are you dealing with it?

_____
_____
_____

Step Family Challenges

The American Academy of Child and Adolescent Psychiatry (2011) explores some of the challenges that stepfamilies face. The members of the new blended family need to build strong bonds among themselves through:

- Acknowledging and mourning their losses
- Developing new skills in making decisions as a family
- Fostering and strengthening new relationships between: parents, stepparent and stepchild, and stepsiblings
- Supporting one another
- Maintaining and nurturing original parent-child relationships

In *Helping Children Adjust*, the Mayo Clinic suggests additional factors to help your children adjust:

- Nurture existing family relationships
- Encourage respect

Which of the actions, above, is your blended family doing?

_____

_____

_____

Which are you actively doing to help your child?

_____

_____

_____

Tips for stepfamilies:

Reading the tips below for step families, identify which ones you are doing, and those that may need more effort.

1. Relationships take time. The average stepfamily takes longer to bond than anyone would like. But accepting this will help. The difficulties you are having are likely a typical stepfamily stage. It helps not to take it personally, even though this is easier said than done.

2. The relationship between biological parents and their children is very different than that between stepparents and stepchildren. In spite of your best intentions, your stepchildren may not immediately love or even like you. You may also find that your feelings are different than you expected, or have changed after you remarried. You cannot force love.

3. You must acknowledge the children's primary bond with their biological parents, no matter what personal feelings or opinions you have of them. You may many times be tempted to undermine or intrude into the relationship between your stepchildren and their biological parents. You may rationalize this is for their own good. Don't kid yourself. Back off.

4. Take time to develop positive relationships before disciplining. Be supportive of the biological parent's discipline. Be willing to take a back seat instead of trying to be in the driver's seat.

5. Make sure visiting stepchildren have a place in your home to call their own.

6. Take one on one time with your stepchildren. You can't create a bond in a group. Take time just for the marriage also.

7. Treat all family members with respect. Yes, even when you are not being treated the same way.

8. Educate yourself about stepfamily life and stages. The library has many books on the topic. Seek outside help before problems

are out of control. Don't be stubborn and pretend you have to handle this all by yourself or perfectly. (adoption.com, n.d.)

Single parenting

Single parent families are headed by mothers, fathers and by grandparents raising their grandchildren. Being the primary caretaker creates the challenge of trying to be both a mother and father to your children. You obviously cannot be both. Remember, a child needs unconditional love from one consistent, caring adult to feel accepted, valued and be well adjusted. That is you!

But, being a single parent can be one of life's biggest challenges. "There are many single parents doing a magnificent job raising their kids, but it is harder to do." (Former President Bill Clinton). Any single parents reading this knows how hard their job is.

Life in a single parent household can be stressful for the adult and the children. Members may expect that the family can function like a two parent family, and may feel that something is wrong when it cannot. The single parent may feel overwhelmed by the responsibility of caring for children, working outside the home and taking care of the house.

In addition, single parent families may have to deal with other challenges that nuclear families do not have to face, such as:

- Visitation and custody problems
- The effects of continued conflict between the parents
- Less opportunity for parents and children to spend time together
- Effects of the breakup on children's school performance and peer relations
- Disruptions of extended family relationships
- Problems caused by the parents dating and entering new relationships (American Psychological Association, n.d., p 1)

Obviously, the burden on single parents can create extreme levels of stress for the parent and the entire family. But, (the good news!) there are ways to reduce the levels and effects of stress.

The American Academy of Pediatrics (2012) suggests ways to reduce the stress of single parenting:

- Keeping a daily routine
- Maintaining consistent discipline
- Keep open communication with your children
- Take the time to enjoy your family
- Take time for yourself

Which of the ways, above, are you practicing to reduce the level of stress in your life?

_____

_____

_____

Which would you like to add?

_____

_____

_____

Due to the added pressure of parenting alone, single parents need to take extra care to reduce their stress levels. This will have benefits not only for the parent, but also for the levels of stress the children experience as well. If you are a single parent, you may be thinking, "I would love to have and feel less stress. But, I have no time to relax and reduce my stress; I have too much to do and too many demands on my time." Actually, like the parent in an airplane who must first place their own oxygen mask over their own mouths before helping their child with theirs, you need to take care of yourself in order to parent well. You and your children ultimately pay a big price when you are never refreshed, relaxed or able to take care of your own needs.

In addition to the suggestions above, in order to reduce your level of stress for certain periods of your life, you may consider lowering your expectations in certain nonessential areas (like cooking homemade meals, volunteering at your child's school, planning elaborate holiday events, etc.) and also asking for help. Remember you are a better parent when you have support and have taken care of your needs, too. It also teaches your children that it is OK to take care of themselves and ask for help when they need it.

How do you take care of some of your needs?

_____

_____

_____

How have you received help or reached out to ask for help?

_____

_____

_____

Are there expectations for yourself or for your children that you have changed since becoming a single parent? What are they?

_____

_____

_____

Understanding what you can provide for your child will help you so that you can enlist other supportive adults who can provide what you

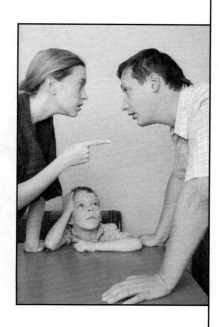

cannot. As a mother and father each bring important and different parenting to a child's development, if you are primarily parenting alone, you may want to find supportive others to fill in gaps that you are not able to provide.

In seeking out supportive others, it may be helpful to define that person as a caring, loving adult that is a positive role model and that is available to have a relationship with your child.

Who is there that has or could have this type of relationship with your child?

_____

_____

_____

What "parents" have you had in your life other than your biological parents? (Another word that may be helpful in understanding the concept of having additional "parents" is "mentor".)

_____

_____

_____

How did those mentors support you? What impact did they have on your life?

_____

_____

_____

It is important to be grateful that you have had those people in your life. Realize that there are other adults who can provide additional support and mentoring in your child's life. Mentoring another person is rewarding for both the mentor and the mentee. Don't be afraid to ask – mentoring another person is an honor. If you don't have a mentor for your child and you think he may benefit from having one, who do you think might be able to do that?

_____

_____

_____

Remember, parents start children on their journey, but the world provides many others who will help your children grow.

Appendix

I. Resources for More Information
II. References

I. Resources for More Information

Tool # 1 Parenting Basics –Things you should know

For a basic overview of some of the laws that apply to children, and parents' rights and responsibilities. From the State Bar of California and the California Bar Foundation's publication *Kids & the Law: An A to Z Guide for Parents,* 2010.
www.calbarfoundation.org

If you need help, or if a child needs help, contact your local county welfare office via this list: Child Protective Services (CPS) Hotlines for each California county, or consult the county listings in your telephone directory. Orange County: 1 714 940-1000 or 1 800 207-4464.
http://www.childsworld.ca.gov/res/pdf/CPSEmergNumbers.pdf

Do you know what the warning signs of child abuse are? Learn how to recognize, prevent and report child abuse. http://www.helpguide.org/mental/child_abuse_physical_emotional_sexual_neglect.htm

To learn about what happens when someone makes a report about the safety of your child, when the police or a social worker must investigate, and when the court gets involved so your child will be safe and protected. http://www.courts.ca.gov/selfhelp-childabuse.htm

2-1-1 Orange County offers information and a referral system linking Orange County residents to community health and human services and support. Either dial 2-1-1 or http://www.211oc.org/.

Parenting.org is a free online resource that provides practical, skill-based materials and information for parents and caregivers of children of all ages.

Tool # 2 Understanding Your Child

For information on important milestones and age and stages of children. See www.healthychildren.org from the American Academy of Pediatrics.

Here are checklists of traits of the different stages. Looking them over will give you a sneak preview of what is to come if your child is still a baby; if your child is older, it should help give you some idea of normal development. Remember, though, that children do have many individual differences in the way they develop. http://cwla.org/positiveparenting/stages.htm

For understanding what is child development, a developmental milestone and the typical milestones or skills that children learn at different ages. www.howkidsdevelop.com

For information on the Erik Ericson's stages of social –emotional development in children and teenagers, see http://www.childdevelopmentinfo.com/development/erickson.html

The AACAP (www.aacap.org) developed Facts for Families to provide concise and up-to-date information on issues that affect children, teenagers, and their families. See Information on normal development during early and late adolescence; see Facts for Families, Adolescent Development #57, #58.

A helpful and easy to read resource in understanding basic temperaments is Taylor Hartman's *The Color Code-A New Way to See Yourself, Your Relationships, and Life* (Simon and Schuster, 1998).

For understanding the nine characteristics that make up a child's temperament, see Mary Sheedy Kurcinka in *Raising Your Spirited Child Rev Ed: A Guide for Parents Whose Child Is More Intense, Sensitive, Perceptive, Persistent, and Energetic* (New York: Harper Collins, 2006)

California's Protection & Advocacy System
Toll Free 800.776.5746 / TTY 800.719.5798;
http://www.disabilityrightsca.org/

Child Mind Institute
The Child Mind Institute is dedicated to transforming mental health care for children everywhere. Founded by Dr. Harold S. Koplewicz and Brooke Garber Neidich, our organization is committed to finding more effective treatments for childhood psychiatric and learning disorders, building the science of healthy brain development, and empowering children and their families with help, hope, and answers. http://www.childmind.org/

Comfort Connection Family Resource Center
The Comfort Connection Family Resource Center at Regional Center of Orange County (RCOC) connects families who have children with special needs to resources and support. Most of Comfort Connection's staff are parents of children with developmental disabilities, and many are bilingual. http://www.rcocdd.com/frc/ccfrc/
Phone: (714) 558-5400; Toll Free: (888) 372-2229 (888-FRC-BABY)

Just One of the Kids: Raising a Resilient Family When One of Your Children has a Physical Disability Authors Kay Harris Kriegsman, Ph. D and Sara Palmer, Ph.D. (Baltimore, MD: The Johns Hopkins University Press, 2013)

Kids in the Syndrome Mix of ADHD, LD, Autism Spectrum, Tourette's Anxiety, and More: The one stop guide for parents, teachers and other professionals. Author Martin L. Kutscher, MD (Philadelphia, PA: Jessica Kingsley Publishers, 2014)

Parent Training
One of Regional Center of Orange County's (RCOC) primary roles is to connect parents with resources and service providers that can meet the individualized needs of their child with developmental disabilities. RCOC organizes a range of workshops, seminars and training session for parents new to the regional center, as well as those seeking advanced learning opportunities.
Contact your Service Coordinator or RCOC's Health Resources Coordinator at (714) 796-5223 for additional information regarding dates, times and locations, and to register.
http://www.rcocdd.com/frc/parent-training/

Reasons for Concern
This information may help to relieve or confirm any concerns you ma have about your child's development.
http://www.dds.ca.gov/earlystart/docs/ReasonsForConcern_English.pdf

Team of Advocates for Special Kids
(TASK) is a nonprofit charitable organization whose mission is to enable individuals with disabilities to reach their maximum potential by providing them, their families and the professionals who serve them with training, support, information, resources and referrals, and by providing community awareness programs. TASK serves families of children aged birth to 26 years of age under IDEA and other systems mandated to provide services to individuals with disabilities. TASK provides advocacy information, workshops and information in Englis and Spanish.
(866) 828-8275 (toll-free in California) (714) 533-8275 (Orange County, CA)
http://www.taskca.org/

For key insights into birth order to help readers understand themselve and improve their marriage, parenting, and career skills see Dr. Kevin Lemans' *The New Birth Order Book: Why You Are the Way You Are* (Grand Rapids, MI: Revell, 2009)

For various articles on understanding family dynamics.
http://www.healthychildren.org/english/family-life/family-dynamics/Pages/default.aspx

For understanding adolescence and keeping your sanity as a parent, read Michael Bradley, M.D.'s *Yes, Your Teen is Crazy! Loving Your Kid without Losing your Mind* (Gig Harbor, WA: Harbor Press, 2003) For signs of involvement gang activity, risk factors and protective factors related to gang activity, see http://www.aacap.org/cs/root/facts_for_families/children_and_gangs.

Tool # 3 Parenting Styles and Loving your Children

On understanding parenting styles, temperaments and how they interact. http://www.aboutourkids.org/articles/parenting_styleschildren039s_temperaments_match

On discovering what kids need to succeed, the Developmental Assets® are 40 common sense, positive experiences and qualities that help influence choices young people make and help them become caring, responsible, successful adults. Because of its basis in youth development, resiliency, and prevention research and its proven effectiveness, the Developmental Assets® framework has become one of the most widely used approach to positive youth development in the United States. http://www.search-institute.org/developmental-assets

For helpful tips to enhance your child's development and useful suggestions that will help you build a loving relationship with your child. www.howkidsdevelop.com

Here some helpful hints to foster a sense of self-worth while protecting a child's self-esteem. http://cwla.org/positiveparenting/tipsesteem.htm

For tips for families and professionals in promoting self-determination in youth with disabilities see: Research to Practice Brief, Improving Secondary Education and Transition Services through Research, April 2003 • Vol. 2, Issue 1; Self-Determination: Supporting Successful Transition. By Christine D. Bremer, Mera Kachgal, and Kris Schoeller http://www.ncset.org/publications/viewdesc.asp?id=962

Tool #4 Role Modeling

For how parents can be a role model for their child learner. http://www.pbs.org/parents/education/going-to-school/supporting-your-learner/role-of-parents/

For how and where to find a positive role model for yourself. http://www.lifegoals.org/how-and-where-to-find-a-positive-role-model/ For information on Anticipatory Guidance, which provide comprehensive, culturally competent, family-centered, community-based child health supervision guidelines consistent with the needs of families and health professionals today. The information contained in the Anticipatory Guidance Cards was excerpted from *Bright Futures: Guidelines for Health Supervision of Infants, Children, and Adolescents*. Bright

Futures http://www.brightfutures.org/anticipatory/index.html

Tool # 5 Empathy

For a perspective on emotions and empathy from a neuroscientist and therapist, especially as they relate to the developing child, see Daniel J. Siegel, M.D., *The Developing Mind* (New York: The Guilford Press 1999).

On the issue of parenting to raise more empathic and emotionally intelligent children, see John Gottman, Ph.D., *Raising an Emotionally Intelligent Child* (New York: Fireside, 1997).

Tool # 6 Communication

Here are some guidelines for making communication with your young child more effective and more fun. Remember, all of these might not be appropriate for all children and all families. You should always consider your cultural standards as well as your own values. *http://cwla.org/positiveparenting/tipscomm.htm*

Tool # 7 Discipline

For a summary of some practical discipline techniques. http://cwla.org positiveparenting/tipsdiscipline.htm

Parenting without Power Struggles: Raising Joyful, Resilient Kids While Staying Cool, Calm, and Connected. This is an extraordinary guidebook for transforming your day-to-day parenting life. Author Susan Stiffelman MFT (Garden City: Morgan James, 2010)

Learn how to set limits and still be a loving parent, bring control to an out-of-control family life, apply the ten laws of boundaries to parenting, definite appropriate boundaries and consequences for your kids... and more. *Boundaries with Kids: How Healthy Choices Grow Healthy Children*, by Dr. Henry Cloud and Dr. John Townsend (Grand Rapids MI: Zondervan, 2001)

A local program for dealing with challenging teens, The Parent Project's *Changing Destructive Adolescent Behavior* is the only program of its kind in the country, in that it focuses on the most destructive of adolescent behaviors. For times and locations go to www.parentproject.com

On the issue of respectfully gaining your child's compliance, see Dr. Kevin Leman's, *Making Children Mind without Losing Yours* (Grand Rapids, MI: Revell, 2000)

From the Children's Hospital of Wisconsin, tips on how deal with ten per tantrums, and how to prevent them. http://www.chw.org/display/PPF/DocID/45130/Nav/1/router.asp

Tool # 8 Stress Management

On Helping Children Handle Stress. This includes: How different children cope with stress and good and bad stress. http://www.healthy-children.org/English/healthy-living/emotional-wellness/pages/Helping-Children-Handle-Stress.aspx

The Boys Town National Hotline'sSM specially trained counselors are available 24 hours a day, 365 days a year to offer you parenting advice and assistance. These dedicated professionals receive ongoing training on how to deal with situations ranging from suicide to challenges parents encounter every day with their teens. Hotline number 1 800 448 3000. http://www.parenting.org/

If you know a child or teen who has experienced a death, this guidebook presents you with simple and practical suggestions for how to support him or her. Learn what behaviors and reactions to expect from children at different ages, ways to create safe outlets for children to express their thoughts and feelings and how to be supportive during special events such as the memorial service, anniversaries and holidays. 35 *Ways to Help a Grieving Child, The Dougy Center for Grieving Children*, 1999.

For more information about the ACE study visit www.acestudy.org or Centers for Disease Control and Prevention at: http://www.cdc.gov/NCCDPHP/ACE/

For symptoms of PTSD in children, see American Academy of Child and Adolescent Psychiatry. (2011) Facts for families. No. 70. *Posttraumatic stress disorder*. http://www.aacap.org/cs/root/facts_for_families/posttraumatic_stress_disorder_ptsd

Tool # 9 Children and Divorce

For basic information on divorce and custody in California, see State Bar of California free online publication, What Should I know about Divorce and Custody? http://calbar.ca.gov/Public/Pamphlets/DivorceCustody.aspx

To find many resources to help you and your children through your separation or divorce. http://www.courts.ca.gov/selfhelp-custody.htm

Talking to children about a divorce is difficult. The following tips can help both the child and parents with the challenge and stress of these conversations: American Academy of Child and Adolescent Psychiatry. (2011) Facts for families. No. 1. *Children and divorce*. http://aa-

cap.org/page.ww?name=Stepfamily%20Problems&section=Facts%20
for%20Families

On adjusting to divorce http://www.healthychildren.org/English/family-
life/family-dynamics/types-of-families/pages/Adjusting-to-Divorce.asp

Tool # 10 Co-Parenting, Step Parenting and Single Parenting

To learn about child custody and parenting time (also called "visitation") cases, how to prepare a parenting plan for you and your children, and how to get or change a court order. And find many resources
to help you and your children through your separation or divorce.
http://www.courts.ca.gov/selfhelp-custody.htm

On keeping your children out of the middle of your co-parenting custody disputes. More effectively manage your difficult shared custody,
joint custody, and co-parenting relationships. The OurFamilyWizard
website® (www.ourfamilywizard.com) is so effective that judges in
nearly all 50 states and 5 Canadian provinces have ordered families to
utilize the site in contested cases to reduce family conflict. http://www
ourfamilywizard.com/ofw/index.cfm/parents/

For sample co-parenting plans, see Emery, Robert, PhD. (n.d) *Truth
About Children and Divorce*. http://www.emeryondivorce.com/parent
ing_plans.php Retrieved from Internet address.

In step families, when parents should consider a psychiatric evaluation
for their child. American Academy of Child and Adolescent Psychiatry
(2011) *Facts for Families. No. 27: Step Family Problems*.http://aacap
org/cs/root/facts_for_families/stepfamily_problems

On Single Parent Families http://www.healthychildren.org/English/
family-life/family-dynamics/types-of-families/pages/Single-Parent-
Families.aspx

References

Adoption.com. (n.d.) 8 tips for stepfamilies.
http://library.adoption.com/articles/8-tips-for-stepfamilies.html Retrieved from Internet address.

American Academy of Child and Adolescent Psychiatry. (2011) Facts
for families. No. 27 *Step family problems*.http://aacap.org/cs/root/
facts_for_families/stepfamily_problems
Retrieved from Internet address.

American Academy of Child and Adolescent Psychiatry. (2011) Facts
for families. No. 70. *Post-traumatic stress disorder*. http://www.aacap

org/cs/root/facts_for_families/posttraumatic_stress_disorder_ptsd

American Academy of Pediatrics. (2004). HealthyChildren.org. *Communication dos and dont's.* http://www.healthychildren.org/English/family-life/family-dynamics/communication-discipline/pages/Communication-Dos-and-Donts.aspx Retrieved from Internet address.

American Academy of Pediatrics. (2004). HealthyChildren.org. *Dealing with sibling rivalry.* http://www.healthychildren.org/English/family-life/family-dynamics/Pages/Dealing-with-Sibling-Rivalry.aspx Retrieved from Internet address.

American Academy of Pediatrics. (2012). HealthyChildren.org. *Stresses of single parenting.* http://www.healthychildren.org/English/family-life/family-dynamics/types-of-families/pages/Stresses-of-Single-Parenting.aspx Retrieved from Internet address.

American Psychological Association, (n.d.) *Single parenting and today's family.* http://www.apa.org/helpcenter/single-parent.aspx Retrieved from Internet address.

Amitay, O. (Radio Interview). (2012) *Sibling rivalry.* TVO Parents. http://feeds.tvo.org/tvoparents

Baumrind, D. (1991). The influence of parenting style on adolescent competence and substance use. Journal of Early Adolescence, 11(1), 56-95.

Block, J., Kemp, G., & Smith, M. (2012). *Help Guide: Children and divorce.* http://www.helpguide.org/mental/children_divorce.htm Retrieved from Internet address.

Bradley, M. (2002) *Yes, your teen is crazy.* Gig Harbor, WA: Harbor Press.

Bright Horizons. (n.d.) *Children and stress.* http://www.brighthorizons.com/talktochildren/stress.aspx Retrieved from Internet address.

California Department of Education. (n.d.) *Social- Emotional development domain.* http://www.cde.ca.gov/sp/cd/re/itf09socemodev.asp Retrieved from Internet address.

Centers for Disease Control and Prevention, *Child Maltreatment Prevention* (Atlanta: National Center for Injury Prevention and Control, 2013). http://www.cdc.gov/violenceprevention/childmaltreatment/index.html Retrieved from Internet address

Centers for Disease Control and Prevention, *Child maltreatment: risk and protective factors* (Atlanta: National Center for Injury Prevention and Control, 2012). http://www.cdc.gov/violenceprevention/childmal treatment/riskprotectivefactors.html Retrieved from Internet address

Centers for Disease Control and Prevention, *Understanding child mal treatment. Fact sheet: Who is at risk for child maltreatment?* (Atlanta: National Center for Injury Prevention and Control, Division of Violence Prevention, 2012). http://www.cdc.gov/violenceprevention/pdf/CM-FactSheet-a.pdf

Cherry, K. (http://psychology.about.com) (2013) *Erikson's psychosocial stages summary chart.* Used with permission of About Inc., which can be found online at www.about.com. All rights reserved. http://psychology.about.com/library/bl_psychosocial_summary.htm Retrieved from Internet address.

Child Welfare League of America (n.d.) *Dealing with the everyday pressures of parenting.* http://www.cwla.org/programs/childprotection childprotectionfaq.htm#dealing
Retrieved from Internet address.

Child Welfare Information Gateway. (2011) *California: what is child abuse and neglect?*
https://www.childwelfare.gov/systemwide/laws_policies/state/index.cfm?event=stateStatutes.processSearch. Retrieved from Internet address.

Cotton, K. School Improvement Research Series, Close up- # 13. (n.d *Developing Empathy in Children and Youth.* http://educationnorthwes org/webfm_send/556. Retrieved from Internet address.

Craig, B. for Between Two Homes®, LLC. (2012). *Children in the middle.*
http://www.childreninthemiddle.com/coparentingplans.htm Retrieved from Internet address.

Crosson –Tower, C. (2008). *Understanding child abuse and neglect* (7th ed.)Boston, MA: Pearson Education, Inc.

Darling, Nancy. (1999, March). Parenting Style and Its Correlates. *Eric Digest, EDO-PS-99-3.* http://ecap.crc.illinois.edu/eecearchive/digests/1999/darlin99.pdf

The Dougy Center for Grieving Children. (1999) *35 ways to help a grieving child.* Portland, OR: The Dougy Center for Grieving Childre

Editorial Projects in Education Research Center. (2011, July 7). Issue A-Z: Special Education. *Education Week.* Retrieved Month Day, Year from http://www.edweek.org/ew/issues/special-education/

Eisenberg, N. 2000. "Emotion, regulation and moral development," *Annual Review of Psychology*, Vol. 51, 665–97.

Epperson, B. (2008) *When Parents of Children with Disabilities Divorce*. Retrieved from http://www.americanbar.org/newsletter/publications/gp_solo_magazine_home/gp_solo_magazine_index/parentsdivorce.html

Findlaw (n.d.) *Child custody basics*. http://files.findlaw.com/pdf/family/family.findlaw.com_child-custody_child-custody-basics.pdf. Retrieved from Internet address.

First Things First.(n.d.). *Importance of a positive male role model*. http://firstthings.org/importance-of-positive-male-role-models. Retrieved from Internet address.

Gottman, J. (1997). *Raising an emotionally intelligent child*. New York, NY: Fireside.

HealthyPlace.com, author Gibson, E. (2012) *General guidelines for parenting or first rule: there are no rules*. Reprinted with permission. http://www.healthyplace.com/parenting/challenge-of-difficult-children/general-guidelines-for-parenting-or-first-rule-there-are-no-rules/ Retrieved from Internet address

Hirschfield, M. (n.d.). *Successful co-parenting*. Reprinted with permission.
http://www.markhirschfield.com/coparenting,%20Mark%20Hirschfield,%20psychotherapy,%20emdr%20therapy,%20san%20francisco.htm. Retrieved from Internet address.
Reprinted with permission.

Iannelli, V. M.D., (2011) *7 Common parenting mistakes*. http://pediatrics.about.com/od/parentingadvice/a/04_ptg_mistakes.htm. Retrieved from Internet address. (http://pediatrics.about.com). Used with permission of About Inc., which can be found online at www.about.com. All rights reserved.

Illnesses and Disabilities, U.S. Department of Health and Human Services, Office on Women's Health (2009) Retrieved from http://www.womenshealth.gov/illnesses-disabilities/parenting/parenting-child-with-disability.html

Keith, K. (n.d.) About.com Guide. Child Discipline Series: *Gain compliance with effective consequences*. http://childparenting.about.com/cs/discipline/a/consequences.htm Retrieved from Internet address.

Kennedy, R. W. (2001) *The Encouraging parent*. New York, NY: Three Rivers Press.

Krause, P. (n.d.) Good Reads. http://www.goodreads.com/ quotes/331077-parenthood-it-s-about-guiding-the-next-generation-and-forgiving-the-last

Kurcinka, M.S. (2006) *Raising your spirited child.* New York, NY: Harper Collins.

Komen, A. & Myers, E. (2000). *Parenting survival kit.* New York, N.Y. The Berkley Publishing Group.

Leman, Kevin, Dr. (2009) *The birth order book.* Grand rapids, MI: Revell.

Maccoby, E.E. & Martin, J.A. (1983).*Socialization in the context of the family: parent- child interaction* .In P. H. Mussen (Ed.) & Hetherington (Vol. Ed.), *Handbook of child psychology: Vol. 4. Socialization personality, and social development* (4th ed., p. 1-101).New York: Wiley.

Mac Kenzie, R. (2001) *Setting limits with your strong-willed child.* New York, NY: Three Rivers Press.

Mate, G. Dr. (Radio Interview). (2011) *Dr. Gabor Mate on diagnosing and coping with ADD.* Allan Gregg TVO. http://ww3.tvo.org/ video/174880/dr-gabor-mate-diagnosing-and-coping-add

Mayo Clinic (2012). *Stepfamilies: how to help your child adjust.* http://www.mayoclinic.com/health/stepfamilies/MY01263/NSECTIONGROUP=2
Retrieved from Internet address.

McCullough, L. Kid Crossing (2007) *The Importance of setting boundaries.* http://kidscrossing.com/documents/Boundaries_000.pdf. Retrieved from Internet address.

McGhee, C. (n.d.) *Divorce and children: do's and don't's.* http://www.divorceandchildren.com/article1.html. Retrieved from Internet address.
Reprinted with permission.

McGhee, C. (n.d.) *Divorce and children: parenting with your ex.* http://www.divorceandchildren.com/article6.html Retrieved from Internet address. Reprinted with permission.

McGhee, C. (n.d.) *Two homes: tips for parenting out of two homes.* *http://www.divorceandchildren.com/article8.html* Retrieved from Internet address
Reprinted with permission.

Niolon, R.(2010). *Step-Families: when families mend.* http://www.

psychpage.com/family/stepfamilies.html Retrieved from Internet address.

Parentkidsright. (n.d.) *Divorce.* http://www.parentkidsright.com/html/divorce2.html
Retrieved from Internet address.

Parenting Guidelines.(2011, Oct. 22.) *Role of parents- be a good role model.* http://www.parenting-guidelines.com/role-of-parents-be-a-good-role-model. Retrieved from Internet address.

Randel, D. & Randel, G., (n.d.) *Boundaries, why are they needed?* http://www.quantumdental.ca/images/boundaries.pdf. Retrieved from the Internet address.

Regoli, R.M, Hewitt, J.D., & Delisi M.(2010). *Delinquency in society.* (8th ed.) Sudbury, MA: Jones and Bartlett Publishers.

Sachs, B. (2001). *The Good enough child.* New York, NY: Harper Collins.

Smith, M. & Segal, J. (2013). Help Guide. *Child abuse and neglect: recognizing, preventing, and reporting child abuse.* http://www.helpguide.org/mental/child_abuse_physical_emotional_sexual_neglect.htm
Retrieved from the Internet.

State Bar of California & The California Bar Foundation (2010) *Kids and the Law: An A to Z Guide for Parents*, pp. 10-11. San Francisco, CA: California Bar Foundation. www.calbarfoundation.org.

Stephenson, M. (2011, March 15.) *Parenting Children with Disabilities.* Retrieved from http://network.crcna.org/disability-concerns/parenting-children-disabilities

Stossel, S. (2013, May). Thanks, mom: revisiting the famous Harvard study of what makes people thrive. *The Atlantic, 22.*

U.S. Department of Health and Human Services Gaudin, J. M., Jr. (1993) Child Welfare Information Gateway. *Child Neglect: A Guide for Intervention 3. Understanding the Causes of Neglect.* https://www.childwelfare.gov/pubs/usermanuals/neglect_93/neglectc.cfm

Vanderbilt, A. (n.d.) Great-quotes.com. Amy Vanderbilt Quotes. http://www.great-quotes.com/quotes/author/Amy/Vanderbilt

Wicks-Nelson, R. & Israel, A.C. (1991) *Behavior disorders of childhood.* Englewood Cliffs, NJ: Prentice Hall.

Wilson, B. (1999) *Creating balance in your child's life*. Chicago, Il
Contemporary Books.

Wooden, J.R. & Jamison, S. (1997). *Wooden: a lifetime of observa-
tions and reflection on and off the court*. New York, NY: McGraw-
Hill Books.

You_didnt_have_a_choice_about_the_parents. (n.d.). *Columbia Wo
of Quotations*. Retrieved May 06, 2013, from Dictionary.com webs
http://quotes.dictionary.com/You_didnt_have_a_choice_about_the_
parents

Zahn-Waxler, C., and others. 1992. "Development of concern for o
ers," *Developmental Psychology*, Vol. 28, No. 1, 126–36.